Editor: Kate Reeves-Brown
Creative Direction & Design:
 Bell Blood Studio
Jacket Design: Bell Blood Studio
Junior Jacket Designer: Amy Cox
Jackets Coordinator: Lucy Philpott
Senior Producer (Pre-production):
 Tony Phipps
Senior Producer: Stephanie McConnell
Creative Technical Support:
 Sonia Charbonnier
Senior Acquisitions Editor:
 Stephanie Milner
Art Director: Maxine Pedliham
Publishing Director: Mary-Clare Jerram

Photographers: Liz and Max
 Haarala Hamilton
Food stylist: Valerie Berry
Prop stylist: Rachel Vere
Make-up artist: Madge Foster

First published in Great Britain
 in 2020
 by Dorling Kindersley Limited
 80 Strand, London, WC2R 0RL

Copyright © Dorling Kindersley
 Limited, 2020
Text copyright © Chris Bavin, 2020
 A Penguin Random House Company
 10 9 8 7 6 5 4 3 2 1
 001–318365–Jan/2020

- - - - - - - - - - - - - - - - - - - -

A CIP catalogue record for this book
 is available from the British Library.
 ISBN: 978-0-2414-3586-1

Printed and bound in Latvia

A world of ideas:
 see all there is to know

www.dk.com

DK | Penguin
Random
House

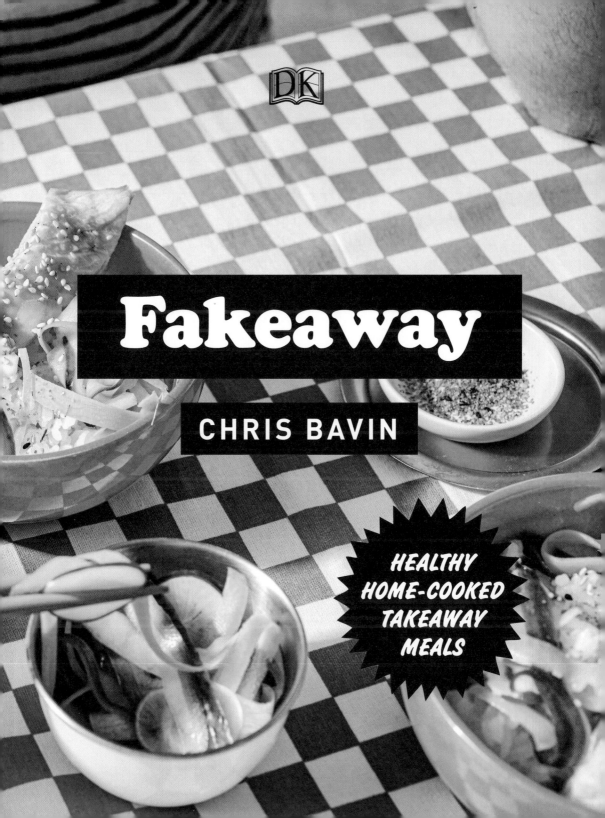

Fakeaway

CHRIS BAVIN

HEALTHY HOME-COOKED TAKEAWAY MEALS

The Recipes

Introduction

Having the opportunity to write another cookbook is such a huge honour and I have loved the process enormously. It has enabled me to try out new recipes, learn about unfamiliar flavours and spend lots of time doing three of my favourite things: cooking, writing and eating!

I really hope you like the recipes and that this book will encourage you to cook a few things that you wouldn't normally try at home, or even get you enjoying cooking more. For me, cooking food and sitting down to enjoy it with family is one of the best things you can do.

Too many of us see cooking as a chore and I think that is such a shame. Part of the lack of enjoyment, or the reason for having lost the love of cooking, normally comes down to worrying about what to have on a daily basis, and having to squeeze it into a packed day. The last thing people want to do is spend precious time cooking a meal, for people not to eat it or enjoy it. For me, the best way to stop cooking from becoming a chore is to write a meal plan. If you know what you are cooking and you know you have all the ingredients to cook it, the whole thing really is a much more enjoyable experience. Furthermore, if you get everyone involved in choosing and selecting the meals they want to eat for the coming few days, then they can't turn round

and say they don't like it or don't fancy that! Plan your meals, write a list and make cooking them fun again!

Get yourself organized, put some music on, pour yourself a glass of cold beer or wine and get the kids involved. Yes, it will be a little slower and messier, but they will love it. Plus, you will be giving them the gift of cooking skills – and that is something that they will appreciate for the rest of their lives!

We all need to be able to cook, and the less we do it the less we want to do it, so let's break that cycle. We love our food, let's love to cook it, too!

TAKEAWAYS & FAKEAWAYS

Not cooking has never been easier. You can get food delivered straight to your door from your local takeaway or eat out at a plethora of restaurants, and all this means we are cooking less and less.

The vast use of fast food outlets is one of the biggest changes I have seen in my lifetime. We hardly ever had any takeaways when I was a kid, and eating out was something reserved for special occasions, but that has all changed. Takeaways, at the end of a long week or when you want a night off from cooking, are fine, but we are having them more often than an occasional treat. When you think about the calories, and the cost, it is so much better to make it yourself.

More often than not, when I get a takeaway (albeit quite infrequently these days), I'm disappointed. By the time you get it, it's going cold and nowhere near as nice as something prepared fresh at home.

I have come up with lots of versions of our favourite takeaways that are quick, easy and full of flavour. The aim is to save your money and your waistline.

I think it's important to point out that I'm not trying to create exact replicas of takeaway dishes, nor be truly authentic to their origins. What I have tried to do is give you the perfect balance of ease, flavour and nutrition. Simple things like baking instead of frying and reducing the sugar, fat and salt means that you can have the pleasure that you get with

eating out or having a takeaway, but without the guilt or the big bill at the end.

Each recipe contains nutritional analysis so you can plan your meals effectively. Keep an eye out for recipes suitable for vegetarians, vegans or those with a dairy or gluten intolerence. But please also be mindful of the ingredients you buy. Some things, such as mustard, prepared sauces, like soy and fish sauce, cheese and stock cubes may not be suitable for all diets and you must take care when you do your shopping.

As I hope you would expect from me, the recipes in this book are not overly complicated; there are no ingredients that you won't be able to find in any local shop. I don't use equipment or techniques that you won't be familiar with, and I always try to keep the ingredients affordable. I have even tried to minimize the washing up!

NOTE

The recipes contained within this book include nutritional analysis based on single servings and signifiers that identify suitability for:

- **V** vegetarian diets
- **VE** vegan diets
- **DF** dairy free diets
- **GF** gluten-free diets

Always check the labels of ingredients to check suitability when cooking or preparing food for those with allergies and intolerances. Take care when sourcing cheeses for vegetarian and vegan diets as many are produced using animal products.

For the healthiest version of these recipes, all minced meat should be lean; yogurt, milk and cream should be low-fat and soy sauce should be reduced-salt.

Taste of India

We have embraced the flavours of India in the UK; we are a nation of curry lovers. Unlike lots of other cuisines, however, we haven't embraced it as much when it comes to cooking it at home. I think lots of us think that it's complicated or difficult to blend different flavours and spices together! Well, the recipes in this chapter are easy, I promise you. Plus, they are full of flavour. They might not be 100% authentic, but lots of the dishes we get from our local Indian takeaway have been adapted for us Brits anyway. I have tried to give you all the enjoyment of this food without all the calories and fat.

You can always make a bigger batch when you cook it, divide it up and have it in the freezer for the next time you fancy a curry... which, if you are anything like me, won't be that far in the future.

This, for me, is a cuisine that doesn't need lots of ghee, cream or fat, as you get incredible flavour and colour from the spices. It can have such freshness and pack a real punch if you want. The other thing I love about the food of India is you can pack it full of lovely vegetables.

Serves 4 / Prep 10 minutes / Cook 35 minutes / 283 kcal, 5.5g fat, 20g carbs, 36g protein

Tikka Masala

One of the most popular curry dishes in Britain, if not the most popular. Apparently it originated in Scotland in the 1970s! This is a much-loved dish because it is flavourful, but not too spicy! Normally finished with cream, I have tweaked it to make it healthier.

INGREDIENTS

1 tbsp vegetable oil
1 large onion, finely sliced
2 tsp curry powder
1 tsp ground cumin
1 tsp ground coriander
1 tsp ground turmeric
1 tsp chilli powder
3 garlic cloves, grated
5cm (2in) piece fresh root
  ginger, grated
500g (1lb 2oz) passata
3–4 chicken breasts, cut
  into large chunks
1 tbsp mango chutney
150ml (5½fl oz) plain
  yogurt
salt
1 tbsp toasted flaked
  almonds (optional)
1 tbsp fresh coriander

METHOD

1. Heat the oil in a large frying pan over a low heat. Add the onion and cook slowly for 10 minutes or until lightly golden brown.

2. Add the spices and cook for 1 minute. Then stir in the garlic and ginger and cook for 30 seconds, before pouring in the passata.

3. Simmer over a gentle heat for 10 minutes. Add the chicken and cook for 10 minutes, or until the chicken is cooked through. Stir in the mango chutney and yogurt. Warm through and season with a little salt.

4. Sprinkle over the almonds, if using, and coriander. Serve with basmati rice.

Serves 4 / Prep 10 minutes / Cook 30 minutes / 260 kcal, 14g fat, 19g carbs, 9.4g protein

Spinach, Chickpea & Aubergine Curry

My wife is vegetarian, and, as a former fruit and veg importer and greengrocer, I think any veggie dish is great! I also think that the spices and flavours you get with the food in India lend themselves perfectly to veggie dishes. The curry itself is vegan, dairy free and gluten-free!

INGREDIENTS

1 tbsp vegetable oil
1 onion, finely chopped
2 tsp ground cumin
2 tsp ground coriander
1 tsp mustard seeds
  (optional)
1 large aubergine, cut
  into 2cm (¾in) cubes
3 garlic cloves, chopped
1 tsp chopped fresh chilli
400g can chickpeas,
  drained and rinsed
200g (7oz) cherry
  tomatoes, halved
400g can coconut milk
300g (10oz) spinach
salt
1 tbsp chopped fresh
  mixed herbs, such as
  parsley, coriander and
  chives

METHOD

1. Heat the oil in a large pan and fry the onion over a low heat for 5 minutes. Stir in the cumin, coriander and mustard seeds, if using. Fry for 1 minute until fragrant, then add the aubergine and coat in the spices. Fry for 2 minutes, then stir in the garlic and chilli.

2. Add the chickpeas, then the tomatoes and coconut milk. Simmer gently for 10–15 minutes.

3. When the aubergine is cooked, stir in the spinach and allow it to wilt. Season with a little salt and top with the fresh herbs. Serve with rice or flatbreads.

Serves 4 / Prep 10 minutes / Cook 45 minutes / 338 kcal, 18g fat, 15g carbs, 27g protein

Lamb Jalfrezi Meatballs

Lamb jalfrezi is a perfect slow-cooked recipe, but sometime we just don't have the time to use cuts of lamb that take time to tenderize. I could use lamb fillet, but it is very expensive, so instead here is a little twist on a lamb jalfrezi: a quick jalfrezi sauce with spicy meatballs.

INGREDIENTS

2 tbsp vegetable oil
1 large onion, chopped
3 garlic cloves, chopped
2 tsp cumin seeds
2 tsp coriander seeds
½ tsp crushed dried
  chillies
½ tsp ground turmeric
2 tsp garam masala
400g can chopped
  tomatoes
1 slice bread
1 tbsp milk
500g (1lb 2 oz) minced
  lamb
3cm (1¼in) piece fresh
  root ginger, grated
1 tsp garam masala
salt
2 green peppers, chopped
  into 2cm (¾in) pieces
pinch of sugar (optional)
1 tbsp chopped fresh
  coriander

METHOD

1. Heat half the oil in a pan and fry the onion until soft. This will take about 3 minutes. Add 2 chopped garlic cloves and cook for 1 minute. Add the cumin, coriander and crushed dried chillies. Cook for 1 minute before adding the turmeric and garam masala. Cook for a further 30 seconds, then pour in the chopped tomatoes. Cook everything on a medium heat for 10 minutes.

2. While the sauce is cooking, remove the crusts from the bread, tear the bread into pieces and soak in the milk. Mix together the lamb, remaining garlic, ginger, bread (give it a mush up with a fork) and garam masala with a good pinch of salt. Divide into 12 meatballs.

3. Heat the remaining oil in a frying pan and fry the meatballs until lightly browned. Add the peppers and fry for 1 minute.

4. Meanwhile, when the tomatoes have cooked out for 10 minutes, blend the sauce until smooth. Add 100ml (3½fl oz) water to loosen it, if needed.

5. Drain off any excess fat from the meatballs, then add the meatballs and peppers to the blended sauce. Cook everything together for 3–4 minutes. Check that everything is sweet enough – add a pinch of sugar, if needed. Season with salt and top with the chopped fresh coriander. Serve with rice.

Beef Madras

Madras is lovely as a slow-cooked dish. If you have the time to do that, then simply make the sauce, add stewing steak and cook it on a low heat for 2 hours. I often don't get in until 7pm and need to eat by 7.30pm, so here is my Madras made with steak – the best of both worlds!

INGREDIENTS

4 rump steaks
2 tsp vegetable oil
1 tbsp grated ginger
2 garlic cloves, sliced
salt
1 tbsp each chopped
  fresh coriander and
  toasted flaked almonds

SAUCE

1 tbsp vegetable oil
2 onions, sliced
1 red pepper, thinly sliced
1 chilli, chopped
2 tsp chopped ginger
1 tsp ground turmeric
2 tsp ground coriander
1 tsp ground cumin
1 tsp mustard seeds
1 tsp cayenne pepper
400g can chopped
  tomatoes
small handful of raisins
juice of ½ lemon

METHOD

1. Place the steaks on a plate and add the oil, ginger and garlic. Turn the steaks over in the marinade so they are evenly coated and set aside.

2. For the sauce, heat the oil in a large frying pan and add the onions and pepper. Cook over a medium heat until soft and starting to turn golden brown, about 5 minutes.

3. Add the chilli, ginger, turmeric, coriander, cumin, mustard seeds and cayenne. Fry for 30 seconds, then add the tomatoes. Stir well and cook over a medium-low heat for 10 minutes until it forms a thick paste. Add 100ml (3½fl oz) water and bring to a simmer.

4. While the sauce is simmering, preheat the grill to a high heat. Place the steaks on a foil-lined baking tray, then grill the steaks for 2 minutes on each side. Once cooked, season the steaks with salt and leave to rest.

5. Add the raisins and lemon juice to the sauce.

6. Spoon 2 tbsp of sauce onto each serving place. Slice the steaks thinly, then place them on top of the sauce. Scatter with the coriander and toasted flaked almonds.

7. Serve with basmati rice and yogurt to help cool things down if needed!

Serves 4 / Prep 5 minutes / Cook 15 minutes / 313 kcal, 18g fat, 9.2g carbs, 27g protein

Prawn Korma

Korma always feels like a slightly more indulgent curry due to its creaminess. My version is slightly healthier than usual, with low-fat coconut milk and lots of the flavour coming from fresh root ginger.

INGREDIENTS

1 tbsp vegetable oil
1 onion, finely sliced
1 red pepper, sliced
2 garlic cloves, chopped
  or grated
6cm (2½in) piece fresh
  root ginger, grated
2 tsp garam masala
1 tsp ground turmeric
400g can coconut milk
1 tsp chopped fresh chilli
1 large courgette, cut into
  1cm (½in) chunks
500g (1lb 2 oz) peeled raw
  king prawns
4 tbsp ground almonds
salt (optional)
2 tbsp chopped fresh
  coriander

METHOD

1. Heat the oil in a pan. Add the onion and fry over a medium heat for 2 minutes until soft. Then add the pepper and cook for a further 2 minutes.

2. Stir in the garlic, ginger, garam masala and turmeric. Cook for 1 minute to cook out the spices, then add the coconut milk and chilli. Bring everything to a simmer and stir in the courgette, prawns and almonds. Simmer gently for 3–4 minutes or until the prawns turn pink.

3. Season with a little salt, if needed, and top with the fresh coriander. Serve with basmati rice.

Serves 4 / Prep 10 minutes / Cook 35 minutes / 488 kcal, 6.4g fat, 82g carbs, 22g protein

Prawn Biryani

This is not the traditional way to cook a biryani, because that just takes too long for a family on the go. It has way too much butter and far too little veg, so I've used a little bit of artistic license on this one to give you the biryani experience with half the hassle.

INGREDIENTS

1 tbsp vegetable oil
1 large onion, finely sliced
2 green peppers, finely sliced
½ tsp ground turmeric
3 tbsp Madras curry paste, or any curry paste
1 tsp chopped fresh chilli
5cm (2in) piece fresh root ginger, grated
2 garlic cloves, grated
350g (12oz) basmati rice
800ml (1¼ pints) hot chicken or vegetable stock
salt
1 lemon
400g (14oz) raw king prawns, peeled and cleaned
1 large courgette, finely diced
1 tbsp fresh coriander, to serve
plain yogurt, to serve

METHOD

1. Preheat the oven to 160°C (140°C fan/325°F/Gas 3).

2. Heat the oil in an ovenproof pan with a lid (a shallow flameproof casserole or ovenproof frying pan will work too). Add the onion and peppers and cook over a low heat for 6–8 minutes until soft and golden brown.

3. Add the turmeric, 2 tbsp of the curry paste, the chilli, ginger and garlic and fry for 1 minute. Add the rice and coat it in all the spices. Pour in the stock, add a pinch of salt and give it a stir. Use a vegetable peeler to remove the peel from the lemon and place the peel in the pan. Cover with a tight-fitting lid and bake in the oven for 15 minutes.

4. Mix together the remaining curry paste and the prawns. Set aside.

5. After 15 minutes, remove the lid and scatter the prawns and diced courgette on top. Bake for 5 minutes more.

6. Remove from the oven and leave to stand for 2 minutes while you cut the peeled lemon into wedges. Serve with the coriander, plain yogurt and lemon wedges.

Serves 2 / Prep 10 minutes / Cook 20 minutes / 532 kcal, 35g fat, 17g carbs, 34g protein

Matar Paneer

Paneer is an unaged cheese used in lots of Indian cooking because it does not melt easily. It happily absorbs flavours and is a perfect meat alternative. Paneer can contain high levels of salt, so, if you prefer, this recipe could serve four people with a couple of side dishes.

INGREDIENTS

1 tbsp vegetable oil, plus
  extra if needed
225g (8oz) paneer, cut
  into 3cm (1¼in) cubes
1 heaped tsp cumin seeds
½ tsp ground turmeric
½ tsp chilli powder
1 tsp garam masala
2 garlic cloves, finely
  chopped
4cm (1½in) piece fresh
  root ginger, grated
1 chilli, chopped
6 large ripe tomatoes,
  roughly chopped, or
  200g can chopped
  tomatoes
salt
100g (3½oz) frozen peas,
  defrosted
2 spring onions, chopped
lemon wedges, to serve

METHOD

1. Heat the oil in a frying pan over a high heat. When hot, add the paneer, then turn the heat down to medium and allow it to brown slightly on all sides. Remove it from the pan and set aside on a plate.

2. Return the pan to the heat and add the cumin seeds (adding a little more oil if needed), turmeric, chilli powder, garam masala, garlic, ginger and chilli. Fry for 1 minute, then add the tomatoes. Warm the tomatoes through and, when soft, squash them with the back of a fork. Add a splash of water (2 tbsp) to loosen the sauce and season with salt.

3. Stir in the peas and fried paneer, and simmer gently for 2 minutes to warm everything through. Scatter over the spring onions and serve with lemon wedges.

Sag Aloo

Spinach is one of my favourite vegetables, followed closely by potatoes... so as you could imagine, this dish is a winner for me. Plus, it's a great way to add some colour and extra vegetables to your plate.

INGREDIENTS

1 tsp ground turmeric
salt
500g (1lb 2oz) potatoes,
  cut into 2cm (¾in)
  chunks
1 tbsp vegetable oil
1 onion, finely sliced
1 tsp cumin seeds
1 tsp brown mustard
  seeds
2 tsp ground coriander
3cm (1¼in) piece fresh
  root ginger, chopped
2 garlic cloves, chopped
1 red chilli, sliced
400g (14oz) spinach
  leaves
2 spring onions, finely
  chopped
plain yogurt, to serve

METHOD

1. Bring a pan of water to the boil. Add the turmeric and a pinch of salt. Add the potatoes and simmer for about 3–5 minutes or until they are almost cooked but not breaking up. Drain well.

2. Heat the oil in a sauté pan with a lid. Add the onion and fry gently on a low heat for 5 minutes until soft.

3. Add the cumin seeds, brown mustard seeds and ground coriander. Fry for 30 seconds, then add the cooked potatoes, ginger and garlic. Turn the potatoes over in the spices and fry for a couple of minutes.

4. Add the chilli to the pan and let that fry for a minute before adding in the spinach. Cover the pan with a lid as this will help to wilt it.

5. Once the spinach has wilted, give everything a good but gentle mix, and season with salt.

6. Top with the spring onions and, if it is the only dish you are eating, serve it with a good dollop of yogurt.

Not Dull Dhal

People always think of dhal as a side dish, but actually it can be a main course on its own. Lentils are extremely good for you and they absorb flavour like little sponges. This is a really lovely veggie dish – and if you swap out the yogurt for coconut yogurt, it can easily be vegan.

INGREDIENTS

120g (4oz) red split lentils
1 tbsp vegetable oil
1 onion, finely chopped
1 tsp ground cumin
1 tsp ground coriander
1 tsp ground turmeric
1 green chilli, finely
  chopped, plus extra to
  serve (optional)
3 garlic cloves, chopped
3cm (1¼in) piece fresh
  root ginger, grated
3 tomatoes, roughly
  chopped
600ml (1 pint) boiling
  water
1 tbsp tamarind paste
  (see note)
salt
2 tbsp plain yogurt

METHOD

1. Place the lentils in a bowl and cover with cold water. Leave them to stand while you start cooking.

2. Heat the oil in a saucepan. Add the onion and cook over a low heat for 5 minutes until soft and golden – this gives you a natural sweetness to the dish.

3. Add the cumin, coriander, turmeric and green chilli. Fry for a minute before adding the garlic, ginger and two of the tomatoes. Stir well, then drain the lentils and add the drained lentils to the pan. Coat them in the spices and then pour over the freshly boiled water. Bring the pan to a simmer and simmer gently for 15 minutes until you have a thick paste. If it gets too thick and starts to catch on the bottom of the pan, simply add more water. Dhal can be thick or soupy, depending on how you like it.

4. Once the lentils are tender, stir in the tamarind paste and season with a little salt.

5. Serve topped with a little extra chopped green chilli, if you like it hot, the remaining chopped tomatoes and the plain yogurt.

★ You can find tamarind paste in the spice aisle of most supermarkets, but if you can't find it, you can add 2 tsp mango chutney and the juice of 1 lemon instead.

Serves 6 / Prep 10 minutes / Cook 35 minutes / 70 kcal, 3.2g fat, 6.3g carbs, 2.9g protein

Onion Bhaji

In my last book *Good Food Sorted*, I used this muffin pan method to cook healthy hash browns. The principle is the same, but this time it's for healthy Indian onion bhaji.

INGREDIENTS

2 tbsp vegetable oil
2 large onions (1 red and
  1 brown onion looks
  great), finely sliced
1 carrot, grated
1 tsp ground turmeric
1 tsp ground cumin
1 tsp ground coriander
½ tsp chilli powder
200g can chickpeas,
  mashed with a fork or
  stick blender
salt
2 eggs, beaten

YOGURT DIP

150ml (5½oz) plain yogurt
1 garlic clove, crushed
salt
pinch of chilli powder

*12-hole muffin tin, greased
  and lined with muffin
  cases*

METHOD

1. Preheat the oven to 180°C (160°C fan/350°F/Gas 4).

2. Heat 1 tbsp of the oil in a large frying pan. Add the sliced onions and fry for 5–10 minutes to allow them to soften. Once soft, spoon the onions into a large bowl.

3. Add the remaining oil to the pan along with the carrot. Fry for 2 minutes, then stir in the spices and chickpeas. Fry for a minute, then add these to the onions. Mix everything together and season well with salt. When it has cooled a little (so that you don't scramble the eggs), stir the beaten eggs into the mixture.

4. Spoon the mixture into the prepared muffin tin and bake in the oven for 20–25 minutes.

5. Mix together the yogurt and garlic, season with salt and sprinkle with chilli powder.

6. Serve the warm onion bhajis with the yogurt dip.

Serves 6 / Prep 10 minutes / Cook 15 minutes / 209 kcal, 4.7g fat, 31g carbs, 8.2g protein

Quick Dips & Poppadoms

V

INGREDIENTS

vegetable oil
packet uncooked poppadoms

MINT YOGURT DIP

2 tsp mint jelly
150ml (5½fl oz) plain yogurt
¼ cucumber, chopped
black pepper

ONION SALAD

2 tomatoes, deseeded and
 diced
1 small red onion, finely
 diced
1 tbsp chopped fresh
 coriander
1 tsp chopped fresh chilli
juice of ½ lemon

MANGO CHUTNEY

1 tsp vegetable oil
½ tsp mustard seeds
1 tbsp caster sugar
1 tbsp vinegar
1 mango, peeled, stone
 removed and diced
½ tsp ground cinnamon
½ tsp ground coriander

METHOD

1. Use a piece of kitchen paper to wipe vegetable oil over both sides of each poppadom.

2. Place the oiled poppadoms in the microwave, one at a time, and cook on a high heat for 40 seconds (although timings will vary depending on the strength of your microwave). You will see them puff up. If they haven't all puffed up, they may need an extra 10 seconds

3. For the mint yogurt dip, place the mint jelly in a bowl and mix it with a spoon to break it up. Add the yogurt and cucumber, and season with black pepper.

4. For the onion salad, mix everything together in a separate bowl with a pinch of salt.

5. For the mango chutney, heat the oil in a small pan and add the mustard seeds. Allow them to splutter for 20 seconds before sprinkling in the sugar and a pinch of salt. When the sugar turns golden brown, add the vinegar – take care as this will splutter. Next, add the chopped mango and turn the heat down to a medium-low heat and cover with a lid. Cook for 5 minutes, giving it a stir every now and then until the mango is soft. Sprinkle in the cinnamon and coriander, stir well and cook for another 2 minutes, then leave to cool and serve.

Serves 8 / 175 kcal, 5.2g fat, 26g carbs, 4.3g protein

Garlic & Coriander Chapatti

INGREDIENTS

300g (10oz) chapatti flour, or 150g (5½oz)
  plain flour and 150g (5½oz) wholemeal
  flour
1 tsp fine salt
1 tbsp vegetable oil
180ml (6fl oz) warm water
30g (1oz) butter
1 garlic clove, crushed
1 tbsp chopped fresh coriander

METHOD

1. Place the flour(s) in a bowl with the salt
   and oil. Add enough warm water to
   bring it together to form a soft dough
   that's not sticky. Knead for 5 minutes.

2. Divide the dough into eight pieces, then
   roll them out into round discs about
   2mm (¹⁄₁₆in) thick, stacking them
   between sheets of baking parchment.

3. Heat a large frying pan over a medium
   heat. Cook the chapattis, one at a time,
   for 30 seconds on each side or until
   they start to brown. Remove from the
   pan and keep warm on a plate, loosely
   covered with foil, while you repeat with
   the remaining chapattis.

4. Melt the butter in a small bowl in the
   microwave and stir in the garlic and
   coriander. Lightly brush each chapatti
   with the butter and then serve.

Serves 4 / 471 kcal, 3.9g fat, 94g carbs, 13g protein

Mushroom & Pea Pilau Rice DF GF V

INGREDIENTS

1 tbsp vegetable oil
1 small onion, finely chopped
1 cinnamon stick, 2 cardamom pods
 and 5 cloves
½ tsp ground turmeric
300g (10oz) chestnut mushrooms, sliced
450g (1lb) basmati rice
600ml (1 pint) chicken or vegetable stock
100g (3½oz) frozen peas, defrosted

METHOD

1. Heat the oil in a saucepan (which has a
   lid), add the onion and cook over a low
   heat for 5 minutes. Add the cinnamon,
   cardamom, cloves and turmeric.

2. Give everything a good stir, then add
   the mushrooms. Fry for 2 minutes until
   the mushrooms start to soften.

3. Stir in the rice and coat it in the spices.
   Pour over the stock. Give it one quick
   stir, cover with a lid, bring it to the boil,
   then turn it down to a gentle simmer.

4. Simmer for 5 minutes, then scatter
   over the peas (add a splash more stock
   if needed), replace the lid and simmer
   until the stock has been completely
   absorbed. Remove the pan from the
   heat and leave it to stand for 5 minutes.
   Use a fork to fluff up the grains of rice,
   and serve.

Chinese Canteen

Before I got a taste for more spicy foods, I always opted for a Chinese. I haven't had one for ages now, or a good one for even longer than that. But I love Chinese food. I think that sweet and sour combination is great; it's so rich and flavourful.

The joy of Chinese cooking is that it's fast. Often dishes are cooked in a really hot wok or frying pan, and the veggies are cooked for only a short time to keep them crunchy and full of vitamins, which always makes the meal look amazing as the veg keeps its colour.

Serves 4 / Prep 10 minutes / Cook 5 minutes / 437 kcal, 7.5g fat, 49g carbs, 39g protein

Chicken Chow Mein

I love this mixture of noodles and crispy veg. It can be a main or a side, and always goes down really well with the kids. It can easily be adapted to be vegetarian, and we often do! If you want to make it gluten-free, use rice noodles and substitute tamari for the soy sauce.

INGREDIENTS

salt
200g (7oz) dried egg
  noodles
1 tbsp vegetable oil
3 chicken breasts, thinly
  sliced
2 carrots, thinly sliced
1 red pepper, thinly sliced
100g (3½oz) mangetout,
  thinly sliced
250g (9oz) beansprouts
4 spring onions, sliced
1 tbsp sesame seeds

SAUCE

2 garlic cloves, crushed
3cm (1¼in) piece fresh
  root ginger, grated
2 tbsp tomato ketchup
2 tbsp soy sauce
2 tbsp oyster sauce
1 tsp rice wine vinegar
  or white wine vinegar

METHOD

1. Put all the sauce ingredients into a jam jar, seal and shake well to combine. Set aside.

2. Bring a pan of salted water to the boil. Add the noodles and cook according to the packet instructions. Drain well and run under cold water to cool. Set aside.

3. Heat a wok or large frying pan on a high heat. Add the oil, then the chicken breasts. Stir-fry for 1 minute, before adding the carrots and pepper. Cook for a minute, then pour in the sauce. Keep everything moving in the pan to prevent it from sticking and burning. Once everything is coated in the sauce, add the mangetout, beansprouts and cooked noodles. Cook for a further minute. You want all the veggies to remain crunchy, so take care not to overcook them.

4. Serve in warm bowls and top with the sliced spring onions and sesame seeds.

Serves 4 / Prep 15 minutes / Cook 10 minutes / 293 kcal, 12g fat, 13g carbs, 32g protein

Beef in Black Bean Sauce

If you have the time to visit a Chinese supermarket, you can buy black beans to make your own black bean sauce, but most of us don't have the time to do this! Here is one of my cheats where I use a jar of shop-bought sauce and simply jazz it up.

INGREDIENTS

500g (1lb 2oz) best-quality beef steak
1 tbsp cornflour
salt and pepper
2 tbsp sesame oil
1 white onion, finely sliced
1 red pepper, finely sliced
1 green pepper, finely sliced
1 small head of broccoli, broken into small florets
3cm (1¼in) piece fresh root ginger, grated
2 garlic cloves, finely sliced or crushed
5 tbsp black bean sauce
1 tbsp rice wine vinegar
1 red chilli, finely chopped
1 tsp sugar
1 tbsp chopped fresh coriander

METHOD

1. Cut the steak into thin strips and mix them in a bowl with the cornflour and some salt and pepper.

2. Heat half the sesame oil in a large frying pan or wok – get it nice and hot as you want the steak to seal as soon as it goes in.

3. Stir-fry the steak for 2–3 minutes on a high heat until sealed and golden brown, then remove it from the pan and set aside.

4. Add the remaining sesame oil to the frying pan and stir-fry the onion for 2–3 minutes, then add the peppers and broccoli and stir-fry for another 3 minutes.

5. Add the ginger and garlic and cook for 1 minute, then add the black bean sauce, rice wine vinegar, chilli and sugar. Add the steak back to the pan and stir everything together. Add 2 tbsp water to loosen the sauce, bring it to a simmer and then top with the coriander. Serve with rice.

Serves 4 / Prep 10 minutes / Cook 5 minutes / 122 kcal, 3.4g fat, 11g carbs, 11g protein

King Prawns with Ginger & Spring Onions

DF

Prawns are often best with lighter sauces like this one, so you get the natural sweetness of the prawns coming through. I love loads of ginger, as it gives it a nice hit. Serve with rice or noodles or just on its own.

INGREDIENTS

1 tsp cornflour
3 tbsp mirin (rice wine)
3 tbsp oyster sauce
2 tbsp soy sauce
1 tbsp sesame oil
20 peeled raw king prawns (frozen are perfect, just defrost before cooking)
5 spring onions, sliced
125g (4½oz) baby corn, sliced in half
125g (4½oz) mangetout, sliced in half
1 garlic clove, finely chopped or crushed
5cm (2in) piece fresh root ginger, grated
125g (4½oz) bamboo shoots (canned is fine, drained)
1 red chilli, finely chopped

METHOD

1. Place the cornflour, mirin, oyster sauce and soy sauce in a bowl or jar and mix well.

2. Heat the sesame oil in a large wok on a high heat (a large frying pan will work if you don't have a wok). Add the prawns, spring onions, baby corn and mangetout and stir-fry for 1 minute. Then add the garlic, ginger, bamboo shoots and chilli and stir-fry for another 2 minutes until the prawns turn pink.

3. Add the sauce mixture and stir-fry for another 1 minute, then serve with rice or noodles, if you like.

Sweet & Sour

Sweet and sour from the takeaway always seems to be a brightly coloured, gluey mess. There is nothing fresh about it. Making your own takes less time than ordering and driving to the takeaway to pick it up, and it tastes amazing. Give it a try.

INGREDIENTS

1 tbsp cornflour
425g can pineapple
  chunks in juice, drained,
  but reserve the juice
2 garlic cloves, sliced
3cm (1¼in) piece fresh
  root ginger, grated
1 tbsp soy sauce
1 tbsp light brown sugar
2 tbsp white wine vinegar
3 tbsp tomato ketchup
1 tbsp vegetable oil
500g (1lb 2 oz) pork fillet,
  thinly sliced, or 3
  chicken breasts, sliced,
  or 500g (1lb 2 oz) raw
  prawns, peeled and
  cleaned
1 red and 1 green pepper,
  cut into chunks
1 small onion, cut into
  wedges
1 red chilli, thickly sliced
sesame seeds and lime
  wedges, to serve

METHOD

1. Mix the cornflour with a little of the reserved pineapple juice until dissolved, then add the remaining pineapple juice along with the garlic, ginger, soy sauce, brown sugar, vinegar and ketchup. Place in a small saucepan and simmer gently for 5 minutes.

2. Heat the oil in a large frying pan or wok on a high heat. Add the pork, chicken or prawns and stir-fry for 1–3 minutes (depending on the meat), until cooked, then transfer to a plate. Place the pan back on the heat and add the peppers, onion and chilli and stir-fry for 2 minutes. Add the pork, chicken or prawns back to the pan with the sauce and pineapple chunks and bring to a simmer. Once simmering and the meat has warmed through, serve with a sprinkling of sesame seeds and some lime wedges on the side. Serve with rice.

★ Note: You can always loosen the sauce with a dash of water, if it's too thick.

Serves 4 / Prep 15 minutes / Cook 2 hours / 338 kcal, 18g fat, 14g carbs, 28g protein

Aromatic Duck Salad

No Saturday night Chinese would be complete without duck. You can serve this as a warm salad, or add a few pancakes and homemade hoisin sauce and roll it up. Make it gluten-free by using rice instead of egg noodles and substitute the soy sauce for tamari.

INGREDIENTS

4 duck legs
1 tsp five-spice powder
salt and pepper
1 tbsp sesame seeds

DRESSING

juice of 1 large orange
2 tbsp each honey, soy
  sauce, sesame oil and
  tomato purée
5cm (2in) piece fresh root
  ginger, grated
2 garlic cloves, crushed

SALAD

bunch of watercress
½ mooli, finely sliced
10 radishes, finely sliced
½ cucumber, finely sliced
handful of fresh coriander,
  finely chopped
bunch of spring onions,
  sliced

METHOD

1. Preheat the oven to 200°C (180°C fan/400°F/Gas 6).

2. Place the duck legs on a large sheet of foil. Sprinkle over the five-spice and some salt. Lay a piece of baking parchment over a large piece of foil and wrap the legs up in a foil parcel, then place on a baking tray.

3. Place them in the oven and turn the heat down immediately to 160°C (140°C fan/325°F/Gas 3). Cook for 2 hours. Meanwhile, make the dressing and salad.

4. Mix the dressing ingredients together in a bowl or jar and season with salt and pepper. Mix the salad ingredients together in a large bowl.

5. When the duck legs are cooked, remove them from the oven. Remove the skin (as this is extra calories!) and use two forks to shred the meat.

6. Mix the shredded duck, dressing and salad together. Scatter over the sesame seeds and serve.

★ To make duck pancakes, put all the hoisin sauce ingredients into a saucepan and gently heat. You are just trying to melt the peanut butter and mix everything together. Spread a little of the hoisin sauce on a pancake, then top with sliced cucumber and spring onions. Either top with shredded duck or mix the duck with a little of the dressing above, then roll up and enjoy.

HOISIN SAUCE

4 tbsp dark soy sauce
2 tbsp smooth peanut
  butter (you can use
  crunchy, if that's all
  you have)
2 tsp dark brown sugar
1 garlic clove, crushed
1 tsp black pepper
2 tbsp rice wine vinegar
1 tbsp sesame oil

Sticky Tofu

Tofu is a great carrier of flavour. It can be rather bland on its own, but spice it up with ginger, soy, chilli and honey, and it transforms into a sticky, sweet and spicy delight. Serve with rice or noodles or have as a side dish or starter.

INGREDIENTS

grated zest and juice of
  1 lime
2 garlic cloves, crushed
  or finely chopped
5cm (2in) piece fresh root
  ginger, grated
1 red chilli, finely chopped
2 tbsp soy sauce
1 tbsp honey
100ml (3½fl oz) apple or
  orange juice
1 tbsp Dijon mustard
1 tbsp sesame oil
2 x 280g (9½oz) blocks
  tofu, cut into 2cm (¾in)
  squares
handful of sesame seeds
handful of chopped fresh
  coriander
handful of chopped
  spring onions

METHOD

1. Mix together the lime zest and juice, garlic, ginger, half the chilli, the soy sauce, honey, apple or orange juice, mustard and a drizzle of the sesame oil in a large bowl. Add the tofu, toss gently to mix and leave to marinate for 20 minutes to 2 hours.

2. Preheat the oven to 180°C (160°C fan/350°F/Gas 4).

3. Line an ovenproof baking dish with baking parchment, then use the remaining oil to coat the base of the dish. Lay the tofu in the dish and pour over the rest of the sauce marinade, making sure you cover the tofu.

4. Cook in the oven for 45 minutes, basting the tofu with the sauce halfway through the cooking time.

5. Sprinkle over the remaining red chilli and the sesame seeds, coriander and spring onions, and serve.

Serves 4 / Prep 5 minutes / Cook 2½ hours / 269 kcal, 16g fat, 13g carbs, 18g protein

Sticky Ribs

This is a great recipe with loads of lovely flavour, but to really get that flavour infused through the ribs, you will need to marinate the ribs for a good few hours, overnight is best. You can then cook them on the barbecue or in the oven. But I promise it will be worth the wait!

INGREDIENTS

750g (1lb 10oz) pork loin
 (baby back) ribs
handful of sesame seeds,
 to finish

MARINADE

3 tbsp soy sauce
2 tbsp honey
grated zest and juice of
 1 lime
2 garlic cloves, crushed
1 tsp five-spice powder
1 tbsp rice wine vinegar
2 tbsp tomato ketchup
3cm (1¼in) piece fresh
 root ginger, grated
1 tbsp sesame oil

METHOD

1. To make the marinade, mix all the ingredients together. Rub the marinade all over the ribs. Put them in a roasting tray to marinate in the fridge, ideally overnight or for at least for 3–4 hours.

2. Preheat the oven to 150°C (130°C fan/300°F/Gas 2).

3. Cover the tray tightly in foil and cook the ribs in the oven for 2 hours 10 minutes.

4. Remove the foil, take the ribs out and spoon out any sauce left in the bottom of the tray, then return the ribs to the tray. Turn the oven up to 200°C (180°C fan/400°F/Gas 6). Put back in the oven, uncovered, for 20 minutes.

5. Cut the ribs up and sprinkle the sesame seeds on top.

Serves 4 / Prep 20 minutes / Cook 20 minutes / 247 kcal, 7.6g fat, 37g carbs, 5.1g protein

Healthy Spring Rolls

Filo pastry is a secret weapon when it comes to cooking healthy pastry dishes. It's so light, it is naturally much lower in calories compared to other pastries that are full of butter. With just a little bit of oil, it crisps up perfectly.

INGREDIENTS

100g (3½oz) cooked
  vermicelli rice noodles
1 large carrot, grated
3 spring onions, thinly
  sliced
1 red pepper, very thinly
  sliced
½ tsp five-spice powder
5cm (2in) piece fresh root
  ginger, grated
1 garlic clove, crushed
2 tbsp oyster sauce
4 sheets filo pastry
2 tbsp sunflower oil
1 tsp sesame seeds
sweet chilli sauce,
  to serve

METHOD

1. Preheat the oven to 180°C (160°C fan/350°F/Gas 4).

2. Place the noodles, carrot, spring onions, pepper, five-spice powder, ginger, garlic and oyster sauce in a large bowl.

3. Place the filo sheets on a work surface in a landscape position. Then cut in half down the middle, giving you eight nice rectangular sheets.

4. Take one sheet at a time and place some of the noodle mixture along the short side. Brush the edges of the sheet with oil, then fold in the edges and roll it up. Brush the outside with oil and place it on a baking tray. Repeat with the remaining pastry and filling.

5. Bake in the oven for 20 minutes or until golden brown. Sprinkle over the sesame seeds, then serve with sweet chilli sauce for dipping.

Serves 2–4 / Prep 15 minutes / Cook 15 minutes / 263 kcal, 10g fat, 20g carbs, 22g protein (based on 2 servings)

Light & Crispy Prawn Toast

This recipe is really best done in a blender, so that you get a nice paste with the prawns. Slightly stale bread works really well here, so use up the less-than-perfect pieces of bread in the bread bin for this recipe.

INGREDIENTS

150g (5½oz) raw prawns, peeled and cleaned
1 garlic clove, sliced
1cm (½in) piece fresh root ginger, grated
1 egg, separated
a pinch of caster sugar
1 tsp light soy sauce
2–3 spring onions, sliced
2 slices bread
2 tsp sesame oil
1 tsp mixed sesame seeds

METHOD

1. Preheat the oven to 180°C (160°C fan/350°F/Gas 4).

2. Place the prawns, garlic, ginger, egg white, caster sugar and soy sauce in a food processor and blitz to a paste. Then stir through the spring onions.

3. Brush the bread on both sides with a little sesame oil. Divide the prawn mixture between the two pieces of bread, then spread it out. Beat the egg yolk and brush it over the top of the prawn mixture. Sprinkle with the sesame seeds.

4. Place the topped pieces of bread on a baking tray and bake in the oven for 12–15 minutes. Remove from the oven, cut into quarters and serve.

Serves 2 / Prep 10 minutes / Cook 10 minutes / 479 kcal, 18g fat, 51g carbs, 24g protein

Egg-fried Rice with Oyster Sauce Pak Choi (DF)

For this veggie-packed recipe I am using brown rice, but you could use long-grain white rice, if you prefer. This can be made to sit alongside other dishes or it can be a meal in one, especially if you add a piece of chicken or some shredded duck (see page 40).

INGREDIENTS

1 tbsp vegetable oil
1 red pepper, finely diced
200g (7oz) mushrooms,
 cut into quarters
250g (9oz) brown rice,
 cooked according to the
 packet instructions
3 eggs, beaten
3 spring onions, chopped
100g (3½oz) frozen peas,
 defrosted
100g (3½oz) canned or
 frozen sweetcorn,
 defrosted if frozen
1 tbsp soy sauce
1 tsp sesame oil (optional)

PAK CHOI

1 tsp vegetable oil
1 garlic clove, sliced
2 pak choi, halved
2 tbsp oyster sauce or
 hoisin sauce
1 tsp sesame seeds

METHOD

1. Heat the vegetable oil in a frying pan, then add the pepper and mushrooms. Fry for 2 minutes. Add the rice to the pan and cook for 1 minute. Move the rice to one side of the pan and add the eggs to the other. As they start to set, mix the rice back into the eggs, allowing it to break up.

2. Add the spring onions, peas and sweetcorn, then season with the soy sauce and sesame oil, if using. Fry for 2 minutes until everything is warmed through.

3. For the pak choi, heat a smaller frying pan on a medium-high heat. Add the oil and garlic, then add the pak choi. Fry for 1 minute, then stir in the oyster or hoisin sauce. Cook for 1 minute, then sprinkle with the sesame seeds. Serve with the egg-fried rice.

Thai Café

My eldest son loves Thai food, and he is 7. This just goes to show how things have changed and how varied the food we have available to us now is. I think I was well into my twenties before I tried any Thai food, but it was love at first taste. For me it feels a bit of a cross between Indian and Chinese food in terms of the flavours – and that is an amazing combination. Thai food has more heat than you normally get with Asian food, and that wonderful balance of light freshness with a real depth of flavour and a kick of heat is perfect.

Thai cooking is all about balancing sweet, salty, spicy, bitter and sour flavours. There are potentially a couple of ingredients that you might not be overly familiar with in here, but I have given you some alternatives that will be easier to find!

I'm not trying to replicate the authentic flavours of Thailand, or the restaurants that serve it, I'm giving you quick, easy, tasty and healthy alternatives inspired by the most popular Thai dishes.

Serves 4 / Prep 20 minutes / Cook 30 minutes / 203 kcal, 12g fat, 16g carbs, 4.9g protein

Thai Green Curry

If you want to make your own curry paste, it can be really rewarding. However, I understand that making your own paste is a lot more effort than opening a jar, and unless you have most of the ingredients, the jar is cheaper. Feel free to add chicken or prawns to this recipe.

INGREDIENTS

1 tbsp vegetable oil
1 red onion, sliced
125g (4½oz) green
  beans
2 tbsp Thai green curry
  paste, homemade or
  shop-bought
400ml can coconut
  milk
1 sweet potato,
  chopped and
  parboiled
125g (4½oz) mangetout
100g (3½oz)
  Tenderstem or regular
  broccoli
fish sauce, to taste
lime juice, to taste
a pinch of light brown
  sugar
1 tbsp chopped fresh
  coriander
lime wedges, to serve

METHOD

1. To make the paste, place all the ingredients into a food processor and blitz into a paste.

2. To make the curry, heat the oil in a large pan, add the onion and soften for 4–5 minutes. When softened but not coloured, add the green beans and fry for another 3–4 minutes.

3. Add 2 tbsp of Thai green curry paste and stir for a minute, then add the coconut milk and stir well, mixing the paste into the coconut milk.

4. Simmer gently for 3 minutes, then add the sweet potato. If you are using chicken, add it now. Simmer for 10–12 minutes, then add the other green veg. If you are using prawns, add them now. Cook for 2 minutes until the veg is tender but still retains some crunch.

5. Season with fish sauce, lime juice and a touch of sugar. Top with the coriander leaves and serve with wedges of lime for squeezing over.

CURRY PASTE

5 green chillies
3 shallots
5cm (2in) piece fresh root
  ginger
3 garlic cloves
small bunch of fresh
  coriander, leaves and
  stalks
2 lemongrass stalks
grated zest and juice of
  1 lime
6 fresh kaffir lime leaves
2.5cm (1in) piece galangal
  or fresh root ginger
1 tbsp coriander seeds,
  crushed
1 tsp ground cumin
1 tsp black pepper
2 tsp fish sauce or shrimp
  paste (or use soy sauce
  if vegetarian)
3 tbsp rapeseed oil
pinch of sugar

Serves 4 / Prep 15 minutes / Cook 2 hours / 592 kcal, 29g fat, 32g carbs, 47g protein

Massaman Curry

The first time I had this curry was in the final of *Britain's Best Home Cook*, and, ever since then, I have fallen in love with it. Having said that, it's quite involved and requires lots of ingredients, so I use a pre-made curry paste, which is still delicious, just a lot easier.

INGREDIENTS

400ml can coconut milk
4 tbsp massaman curry paste, homemade or shop-bought
600g (1lb 5oz) stewing steak, cut into chunks or strips
450g (1lb) new potatoes, cut into quarters
1 large onion, sliced
4 fresh kaffir lime leaves, chopped
1 cinnamon stick
1 tbsp tamarind paste
1 tbsp light brown sugar
1 tbsp fish sauce
100g (3½oz) salted peanuts, roughly chopped
1 red chilli, sliced, to serve

METHOD

1. Preheat the oven to 160°C (140°C fan/325°F/Gas 3).

2. To make the paste, place all the ingredients into a food processor and blitz into a paste.

3. Cook this dish either in an ovenproof lidded pan that you can use on the hob or use a frying pan and then transfer the contents into an ovenproof dish with a lid.

4. To your chosen pan, add 2 tbsp of the coconut milk (use the thick part from the top of the can) and 4 tbsp of massaman curry paste and fry for 1 minute, then add the beef and fry until the beef is coated in the paste and sealed.

5. Stir in the remaining coconut milk, the potatoes, onion, lime leaves, cinnamon, tamarind paste, sugar, fish sauce, half of the peanuts and 200ml (7fl oz) water. Bring to a simmer, then cover and transfer to the oven (or transfer into an ovenproof dish). Cook for 2 hours.

6. Top with the remaining peanuts and the sliced chilli. Serve with jasmine rice.

CURRY PASTE

125g (4½oz) dry-roasted
  unsalted peanuts
2 shallots
5 garlic cloves
1–2 red chilies
5cm (2in) piece galangal
  or fresh root ginger
1 lemongrass stalk
1 tsp ground coriander
½ tbsp ground cumin
½ tsp whole cumin seeds
⅛ tsp ground nutmeg
½ tsp ground cinnamon
⅛ tsp ground cloves
¼ tsp ground cardamom
2 tbsp fish sauce
1 tsp shrimp paste
1 tsp light brown sugar
1–3 tbsp coconut milk

Serves 4 / Prep 10 minutes / Cook 10 minutes / 292 kcal, 15g fat, 18g carbs, 21g protein

Spicy Pork in Lettuce Cups

DF

This is a great low-carb dish. The lettuce leaves are used almost like little boats ready to be filled with the spicy pork mixture. It has sweet and sour notes, and a good kick from the chilli.

INGREDIENTS

1 carrot, finely chopped into matchsticks and/or a handful of radishes, thinly sliced
1 tbsp caster sugar
1 tbsp rice wine vinegar or white wine vinegar
3 spring onions, finely chopped
1 red chilli, finely chopped
2 garlic cloves, grated
5cm (2in) piece fresh root ginger, grated
2 tbsp honey
1 tbsp soy sauce
1 tsp five-spice powder
1 tbsp oyster sauce
1 tbsp vegetable oil
400g (14oz) minced pork
juice of ½ lime
handful of sesame seeds
2 Little Gem lettuces, leaves separated
pickled carrot, to serve

METHOD

1. Place the carrot matchsticks and/or radishes in a bowl and mix in the sugar and vinegar. Set aside.

2. In a bowl, mix the spring onions, chilli (reserving a little to finish the dish), garlic, ginger, honey, soy sauce, five-spice powder and oyster sauce together.

3. Heat the vegetable oil in a large frying pan on a high heat. Crumble in the minced pork, then use a wooden spoon to break it up into small pieces as it cooks. Cook until the meat is golden brown, then pour in the sauce and fry until reduced so that it coats the meat. Add in a squeeze of lime juice.

4. Spoon the meat into a bowl and sprinkle over the sesame seeds and the reserved chopped chilli. Serve it alongside the lettuce cups and pickled carrot and let everybody fill them themselves.

Thai Beef Salad

When it comes to salads, this is a real winner. Hot and spicy, salty, sweet and sour all in one go, with crunchy veggies and tender steak. Always buy the best-quality steak you can – you can always use less, as the flavour will be so much greater.

INGREDIENTS

500g (1lb 2oz) sirloin
  steak
salt and pepper
1 tbsp vegetable oil
handful of radishes
½ cucumber
4 spring onions
100g (3½oz) mangetout
2 large carrots
handful of fresh
  coriander
toasted pine nuts or
  chopped peanuts,
  to serve

DRESSING

1 shallot, finely chopped
3cm (1¼in) piece fresh
  root ginger, grated
1 garlic clove, finely
  chopped or crushed
1½ tbsp rice wine vinegar
1 tbsp tomato ketchup
3 tbsp soy sauce
grated zest and juice of
  1 lime

METHOD

1. Mix all the dressing ingredients in a bowl or jar with 1 tbsp water and set aside.

2. Make sure the steaks are brought to room temperature before cooking and season them well with salt and pepper. Heat the oil in a large pan on a high heat and cook the steaks for 2–3 minutes on each side, then remove from the pan and rest on a plate. You want the meat to relax and to cool slightly. When rested, slice into thin strips and season again.

3. Finely slice the radishes, cucumber, spring onions and mangetout. Use a vegetable peeler to peel ribbons of carrot and mix it with the other vegetables in a large bowl. Add the sliced steak and the dressing, mix together and top with the coriander and nuts. Serve.

Serves 4–6 / Prep 20 minutes / 158 kcal, 5.1g fat, 19g carbs, 6.0g protein

Papaya Salad

This is the most famous salad in Thailand. It is fresh and light and full of flavour. Green papaya are generally not found in the supermarket, but you can get them at specialist Oriental supermarkets and online. It's worth going to the effort though, as this salad is a gem.

INGREDIENTS

2 garlic cloves
5cm (2in) piece fresh root
  ginger, grated
1 red chilli, finely chopped
  (or less if you don't like it
  too hot)
2 tbsp light brown sugar
3 tbsp fish sauce
juice of 2 limes (about 4
  tbsp)
40g (1½oz) peanuts
200g (7oz) green beans,
  cut into 3cm (1¼in)
  pieces and blanched
1 green papaya, peeled
  and grated
1 large carrot, cut into
  thin matchsticks
3 spring onions, finely
  sliced
large handful of chopped
  fresh coriander
a few mint leaves

METHOD

1. Mix together the garlic, ginger, chilli, brown sugar, fish sauce and lime juice in a jam jar or bowl until the sugar has dissolved.

2. Toast the peanuts lightly in a warm pan, then roughly chop. Set aside.

3. In a large bowl, place the blanched beans, papaya, carrot and spring onions, and mix together. Pour in the sauce and finally stir in the coriander and mint then serve with the peanuts scattered over the top.

★ Swap the fish sauce for soy sauce to make this dish vegan. And remember to always check the labels of sauces when cooking the gluten-free version.

Serves 4 / Prep 15 minutes / Cook 10 minutes / 774 kcal, 26g fat, 78g carbs, 53g protein

Chicken Satay Noodles

Chicken satay skewers are a great starter, but they need something else to turn them into a complete meal. This is my Friday-night family version, where you can use up any veg you have in the fridge.

INGREDIENTS

3–4 chicken breasts, cut into strips
1 tbsp soy sauce
1 tsp cornflour
½ tsp ground turmeric
350g (12oz) dried egg noodles
salt
2 tbsp vegetable oil
1 small red onion, finely chopped
1 garlic clove, crushed
3cm (1¼in) piece fresh root ginger, grated
1 tsp chopped fresh chilli
3 tbsp crunchy peanut butter
2 tbsp sweet chilli sauce
400ml can coconut milk
3 spring onions, sliced
1 green pepper, sliced
handful of mangetout
100g (3½oz) green beans, halved
juice of 1 lime
chopped peanuts and fresh coriander, to serve

METHOD

1. Place the chicken in a bowl with the soy sauce, cornflour and turmeric, mix well and set aside.

2. Cook the noodles in boiling salted water for about 2–3 minutes, then drain. Place the noodles back into the saucepan, add a dash of the oil and toss together. Set aside.

3. Heat the rest of the oil in a wok or large frying pan. Add the onion and stir-fry for a couple of minutes. Add the garlic, ginger and chilli and stir-fry for a further minute before adding in the peanut butter, sweet chilli sauce and coconut milk. Stir until combined, then add in the chicken and simmer for 3 minutes.

4. Add all the veg and simmer gently for a further 2 minutes before stirring in the noodles. Allow them to warm through, then finish with a good squeeze of lime juice and serve with some chopped peanuts and coriander on top. If the sauce thickens too much, simply add a splash of water to loosen it.

Serves 4 / Prep 10 minutes (plus soaking) / Cook 10 minutes / 502 kcal, 19g fat, 54g carbs, 26g protein

Pad Thai

Pad Thai can be found on nearly every Thai restaurant's menu, and you can often judge the restaurant by the quality of its pad Thai. It is actually quite simple and quick to make at home, and it tastes amazing. You can use other types of noodles, if you like.

INGREDIENTS

200g (7oz) dried thick rice
  noodles
1 tbsp fish sauce
1 tbsp tamarind paste
1 tbsp light brown sugar
3 tbsp soy sauce
grated zest and juice of
  1 lime
1 red chilli, chopped
  (optional)
1 tbsp vegetable oil
200g (7oz) raw peeled
  king prawns
5 spring onions, finely
  sliced
2 garlic cloves, crushed
120g (4oz) mangetout (or
  use peppers, green
  beans, broccoli, etc)
200g (7oz) beansprouts
2 eggs, beaten
100g (3½oz) salted
  peanuts, chopped
handful of chopped fresh
  coriander
lime wedges, to serve

METHOD

1. Soak the noodles in warm water for 15 minutes, or until soft but firm in the middle. Drain and set aside.

2. Mix together the fish sauce, tamarind paste, sugar, soy sauce and the lime zest and juice. Add the chopped chilli at this point, if you want it spicy.

3. Heat the oil in a pan and cook the prawns until they are turning pink, then remove from the pan and set aside. Add the spring onions, garlic and mangetout to the same pan and fry for a couple of minutes.

4. Add the drained noodles and the sauce to the pan, along with about 2 tbsp water.

5. Cook on a high heat for 3–4 minutes until the noodles are cooked through and everything is mixed together. Stir in the beansprouts and mix well.

6. Push everything to one side of the pan and add the beaten eggs into the empty side of the pan.

7. Cook the eggs for 2 minutes until the white starts to set, then mix everything together until the eggs are mixed into the veg and noodles.

8. Take the pan off the heat and add the chopped peanuts and coriander. Serve with wedges of lime.

Serves 2 / Prep 15 minutes/ Cook 20 minutes / 596 kcal, 22g fat, 73g carbs, 24g protein

Thai Noodle Soup

This dish can be made even quicker if you make a large batch of the coconut stock and then simply freeze it in portions. When you want a super-quick supper, simply defrost it in a pan and add the prawns or some leftover roast chicken along with lots of veggies and noodles.

INGREDIENTS

1 tbsp vegetable oil
5cm (2in) piece fresh root
  ginger, roughly chopped
1 red chilli, roughly
  chopped
2 garlic cloves, sliced
2 lemongrass stalks,
  roughly chopped
½ tsp ground turmeric
400ml can coconut milk
200ml (3½fl oz) vegetable,
  fish or chicken stock
100g (3½oz) baby corn,
  halved
100g (3½oz) sugar snap
  peas
150g (5oz) dried thick rice
  noodles
150g (5oz) raw peeled
  king prawns or
  shredded cooked
  chicken
½ tsp light brown sugar
a dash of fish sauce
juice of 1 lime
1 tbsp fresh coriander
a few mint leaves

METHOD

1. Heat the oil in a saucepan, add the ginger, chilli, garlic, lemongrass and turmeric. Fry on a medium heat for 1 minute. Pour in the coconut milk and stock and simmer gently for 10–15 minutes.

2. Pass the flavoured stock through a sieve into a clean pan to get rid of all the bits.

3. Place the stock back on the heat and add the baby corn, sugar snaps, rice noodles and prawns or chicken. Simmer gently for 3–4 minutes or until the noodles are soft and the prawns are cooked.

4. Remove from the heat and season with the brown sugar, fish sauce and lime juice. Finish with the coriander and mint, and serve in deep bowls.

Serves 4 / Prep 25 minutes/ Cook 12 minutes / 272 kcal, 11g fat, 9.8g carbs, 34g protein

Thai Fish Cakes

If you have a jar of red or green curry paste in the fridge and you are not sure what to do with the last little bit, you can always add it to this fish mix to give it another flavour boost.

INGREDIENTS

700g (1½lb) white fish, skinned and cut into 2cm (¾in)chunks
6cm (2½in) piece fresh root ginger, grated
2 garlic cloves, grated
1 red chilli, finely chopped
1 egg
3 spring onions, finely chopped
2 tbsp finely chopped coriander
1 tsp light brown sugar or palm sugar
1 tsp fish sauce
1 lime
40g (1½oz) flour
3 tbsp vegetable oil

METHOD

1. Place the fish, grated ginger, garlic, chilli, egg, spring onions, coriander, sugar and fish sauce in a food processor. Grate in the zest of the lime and squeeze in half the juice. Pulse until you have a paste.

2. With slightly damp hands take a spoonful of the mixture, about the size of a golf ball and flatten to form a neat pattie. Lightly dust with flour.

3. Heat the oil in a pan and fry the fish cakes for 2 minutes on eacg side until golden brown. You may need to do this in batches. These are lovely served with a salad of green beans and red onion (see tip below).

★ To make an accompanying salad, blanch 200g (7oz) green beans and place them in a bowl with 1 finely sliced red onion, 1 tsp finely shredded mint and 1 tsp finely chopped red chilli. Make a dressing from the juice of 1 lime, 1 tbsp brown sugar and 2 tbsp fish sauce. Mix everything together and serve.

Serves 4 / Prep 10 minutes / Cook 20 minutes / 436 kcal, 29g fat, 19g carbs, 25g protein

Salt & Pepper Squid

Ok, so this requires shallow-frying, which isn't exactly healthy, but the crispy coating and tender squid with a little kick from the black pepper makes for a marriage made in heaven. They are certainly healthier than the battered deep-fried version.

INGREDIENTS

600g (1lb 5oz) squid hoods (tubes) or calamari, cleaned
2 tsp salt
1½ tbsp black pepper
60g (2¼oz) rice flour (or you can use cornflour)
about 100ml (3½fl oz) vegetable oil
1 chilli, chopped (optional)

DIPPING SAUCE

1 tbsp vegetable oil
1 shallot, finely chopped
2 garlic cloves, crushed
2cm (¾in) piece fresh root ginger, grated
1 red chilli, finely chopped
½ tsp salt
½ tsp sugar
1 tbsp light soy sauce
1 tbsp sweet chilli sauce
1 tbsp tomato ketchup

METHOD

1. First, make the dipping sauce. Heat the oil in a pan, add the shallot, garlic, ginger, chilli, salt and sugar and cook for 5–6 minutes. Add the soy sauce, chilli sauce, ketchup and 100ml (3fl oz) water and simmer for 10 minutes. You can then blitz or blend it to get a smoother consistency, if you like. Set aside.

2. Preheat the oven to 100°C (80°C fan/210°F/Gas ¼).

3. Cut the squid into rings, wash it, then dry it off with some kitchen paper.

4. Mix the salt, pepper and flour together in a large bowl. Add the squid to the flour mixture and make sure it is well coated.

5. Add enough of the oil to a pan to coat the bottom and heat until hot. Dip one of the squid rings in and, if it sizzles, it's ready.

6. Shake off any excess flour and place a few bits of squid into the pan, without overcrowding it, then fry for 1–2 minutes on each side until golden brown.

7. Place onto a baking tray and pop into the oven to keep warm while you cook the rest.

8. Sprinkle over the chopped chilli, if using, and serve with the dipping sauce.

日本

Japanese Joint

I was well into my thirties before I tried sushi and other Japanese food, and I was totally hooked. The clean, fresh flavours, the beautiful presentation and the medley of vibrant colours make it an amazing cuisine. I haven't been to Japan yet, but it is very high up on my list of places to visit when the kids are old enough!

It is thought that Japan has one of the healthiest diets on the planet, and the fact that they have one of the longest living populations really reinforces that! The Japanese diet is thought to have originally been vegan before the introduction of fish. It is still mainly based on fish and vegetables, with very little meat and practically no dairy products, making it low in saturated fat.

The recipes here are a great way to introduce you to the flavours of Japan or to help you on your way to cooking more Japanese-style dishes at home. I can assure you, you are in for a treat.

Serves 2 / Prep 10 minutes (plus cooling) / Cook 5 minutes / 359 kcal, 16g fat, 14g carbs, 37g protein

Teriyaki Steak Salad

Teriyaki sauce is so versatile. It can be made and stored in the fridge for a good few days. It is perfect as a marinade, glaze or even as a dipping sauce.

INGREDIENTS

4 steaks (of your choice)
1 tbsp vegetable oil
salt

SALAD

100g (3½oz) green beans, halved and blanched
100g (3½oz) sugar snap peas
100g (3½oz) frozen peas, defrosted
1 red onion or shallot, thinly sliced
1 avocado, peeled, stone removed and diced
small handful of rocket or watercress
handful of fresh coriander
1 tbsp mint leaves

METHOD

1. Make the teriyaki sauce by gently warming all the ingredients apart from the cornflour in a small pan, just until the sugar has dissolved. Mix the cornflour with 1 tsp water, then remove the sauce from the heat and mix in the cornflour paste. Stir well and set aside until cool.

2. Drizzle the steaks with the oil. Heat a frying pan on a high heat. Add the steaks to the pan – you may need to do this two at a time. Cook for 2 minutes, then turn them over and cook on the other side for 2 minutes, or until cooked to your liking (depending on how thick they are and how you want them cooked). Remove them from the pan and leave to rest. Season with a little salt.

3. Mix all the salad ingredients together in a bowl.

4. Once the steak has cooled, slice it, then add it to the salad. Dress it with enough teriyaki sauce to coat it, then serve.

TERIYAKI SAUCE

1 tbsp light brown sugar
3 tbsp light soy sauce
3 tbsp dark soy sauce
1 garlic clove, crushed
3cm (1¼in) piece fresh
 root ginger, grated
1½ tbsp red wine vinegar
½ tsp Chinese five-spice
2 tsp cornflour

Serves 4 / Prep 30 minutes / Cook 10 minutes / 402 kcal, 14g fat, 48g carbs, 19g protein

Sushi

DF

You can now get everything you need to make your own sushi in the supermarket, so you no longer have to travel into town to get your fix. It's pretty easy to make if you keep it simple – and, better still, the rice can be made and cooled the day before.

INGREDIENTS

300g (10oz) sushi rice
4 tbsp rice wine vinegar
1½ tbsp caster sugar
4 nori seaweed sheets
3 tbsp mayonnaise mixed
  with 1 tsp soy sauce

FILLINGS

½ cucumber, cut into
  slices
100g (3½oz) smoked
  salmon slices
1 avocado, peeled, stone
  removed and cut into
  slices
1 red pepper, cut into
  slices
145g can tuna, drained

TO SERVE

pickled ginger
wasabi
soy sauce

METHOD

1. Cook the sushi rice according to the packet instructions. Mix together the rice vinegar and sugar. When the rice is cooked, stir in the vinegar and sugar, then tip it out onto a tray so that it cools quickly. Once cooled, cover and leave in the fridge.

2. Take a sheet of nori and place it shiny-side down on a sushi mat (they cost about £1 in most supermarkets). Cover three-quarters of the sheet with a layer of rice about 1cm (½in) thick. If you use slightly wet hands, it helps prevent the rice from sticking.

3. Spread a little of the mayo mixture over the rice, then place a line of your favourite filling ingredients down one edge of the rice. Simply use the mat to roll up the nori and rice, making sure that the end of the roll is the plain nori, which you can then dampen very slightly to help it stick and prevent it from unrolling.

4. With the salmon, take a square of clingfilm about 7cm (3½in) square. Place a 7cm (3½in) square of salmon in the centre. Take 1 tbsp of cooked rice and place it on top of the salmon. Bring the edges of the clingfilm up together and twist them to make a ball of rice, then simply unwrap it. Serve with pickled ginger and wasabi if you like it hot. Serve all the sushi with pickled ginger, wasabi and soy sauce.

Japanese Poke Bowl

Poke bowls have become really trendy in recent years. They are traditionally from Hawaii and consist of raw fish served in a bowl with rice and veg, but now they are found in lots of Japanese restaurants, taking advantage of all the amazing fresh fish.

INGREDIENTS

120g (4oz) sushi rice
salt
2 tsp white wine vinegar
1 tsp caster sugar
2 x 125g (4½oz) salmon
  fillets or lightly smoked
  salmon fillets
sesame seeds, to serve

PICKLED VEG

½ cucumber
1 carrot
2 tsp caster sugar
1 tbsp white wine vinegar
1 tsp chopped fresh chilli
4–5 radishes, thinly
  sliced

CHILLI MAYO

4 tbsp mayonnaise
1 tsp Shichimi chilli sauce
  or other chilli sauce

METHOD

1. First make the rice. Rinse the rice in a sieve under cold water for a minute. Then place it in a pan that has a lid. Pour in 200ml (7fl oz) water. Add a pinch of salt. Cover with a lid and place on the heat. Bring the pan to a gentle simmer and simmer for 6–8 minutes or until all the water has been absorbed. Leave it to stand, covered, for 10 minutes, then tip the rice out onto a plate or tray and allow it to cool completely.

2. Mix together the white wine vinegar and sugar in a small bowl, then stir this into the cooled rice. Set aside.

3. Preheat the oven to 190°C (170°C fan/375°F/Gas 5).

4. Wrap the salmon fillets in foil and place them on a baking tray. Bake in the oven for 10–12 minutes, depending on how thick the pieces are. Once cooked, remove from the oven and leave to stand.

5. For the pickled veg, use a vegetable peeler to peel ribbons of cucumber and carrot. Mix together the sugar, vinegar and chilli. Add the vegetables, including the radishes, and mix well. Leave to stand for 10 minutes.

6. Mix together the mayo and chilli sauce in a small bowl.

7. Divide the cooled rice between two bowls. Top with the cooked salmon and pickled veg. Drizzle with the chilli mayo and sprinkle with sesame seeds, then serve.

Serves 4 / Prep 20 minutes / Cook 2 hours / 472 kcal, 14g fat, 54g carbs, 32g protein

Duck Donburi

Donburi means 'bowl' where different elements, whether fish, meat or veg are served on a bed of rice in an oversized bowl. Slow-cooked duck legs are one of the most delicious things to cook at home. After 2 hours in the oven, the meat just falls off the bone!

INGREDIENTS

4 duck legs
1 tsp five-spice powder
2 garlic cloves, lightly
   crushed
salt
200g (7oz) sushi rice
2 carrots, grated
½ cucumber, cut into fine
   matchsticks
6–8 tbsp homemade or
   shop-bought yakitori
   sauce, see below
6 spring onions, chopped
1 tbsp sesame seeds

YAKITORI SAUCE

70ml (2½fl oz) soy sauce
1 tsp finely chopped red
   chilli
2 tbsp brown sugar
1 garlic clove, grated
1 tsp five-spice powder
1 tbsp rice vinegar or
   white wine vinegar

METHOD

1. Preheat the oven to 200°C (180°C fan/400°F/Gas 6).

2. Place the duck legs on a large sheet of foil set on a baking tray. Sprinkle over the five-spice and add the garlic and a good pinch of salt, then cover with the excess foil and seal around the edges to make a parcel. Place in the oven, turn the heat down to 160°C (140°C fan/325°F/Gas 3) and cook for 2 hours.

3. Pour the sushi rice into a measuring jug to find its volume. Give it a quick rinse and place the rice in a saucepan with a tight-fitting lid. Measure out 1½ times the amount of water (so if you have 100ml (3½fl oz) of rice, you will need 150ml (5fl oz) of cold water).

4. Pour the water over the rice, then add a pinch of salt. Cover and bring to a simmer. Simmer for 8 minutes or until all the water has gone. Remove from the heat and leave to stand, covered, for 10 minutes. Use a fork to break up the grains a little, although it will be sticky. Leave the rice uncovered to cool slightly.

5. Use two forks to shred the duck meat from the bone.

6. Divide the rice between four deep bowls, then add a pile of duck, carrot and cucumber. Drizzle over the sauce and then sprinkle with sesame seeds and spring onions. (If you are making your own sauce, simply mix everything together and store in a jam jar.)

Japanese Joint   77

Serves 4 as a side dish/ Prep 5 minutes / Cook 5 minutes / 67 kcal, 1.9g fat, 6.6g carbs, 4.2g protein

Green Veg Stir-fry with Oyster Sauce

Oyster sauce is one of those amazing jarred sauces. It's virtually impossible to recreate at home. Buy a good-quality one though, as they tend to be far more balanced in flavour.

INGREDIENTS

2 tsp chilli oil (or 2 tsp vegetable oil and ½ tsp crushed dried chillies)
handful of Tenderstem broccoli
4 pak choi, cut into quarters
2 garlic cloves, sliced
100g (3½oz) sugar snap peas
4 tbsp oyster sauce
juice of 1 lime

METHOD

1. Heat the oil (or oil and crushed dried chillies) in a large frying pan or wok on a medium heat, then add the broccoli and stir-fry for 1 minute. Add the pak choi and garlic and stir-fry for a further minute.

2. Turn up to a high heat, add the sugar snap peas and a splash of water (1 tbsp), which will help to steam them. Once the water has evaporated, add the oyster sauce and warm through.

3. Serve the veg while still crunchy with a good squeeze of lime at the last minute.

Serves 4 / Prep 20 minutes / Cook 30 minutes / 829 kcal, 19g fat, 103g carbs, 60g protein

Chicken Katsu Curry

If you have ever ventured into a Japanese restaurant, this will be on the menu. Crispy coated chicken with a mildly spicy curry sauce – it's a curry that the whole family will love. I use chicken breasts here, but boneless thigh fillets also work well.

INGREDIENTS

4 chicken breasts
salt and pepper
2 eggs, beaten
75g (2½oz) plain flour
150g (5oz) breadcrumbs
1 tsp ground turmeric
½ tsp curry powder
2 tsp vegetable oil
300g (10½oz) basmati rice
1 tbsp rapeseed oil
1 onion, finely chopped
1 carrot, finely copped
2 garlic cloves, crushed
1 tbsp curry powder
1 tsp garam masala
50g (1¾oz) smooth
  peanut butter
400ml (14fl oz) chicken
  stock
5 spring onions, sliced
1 red chilli, finely sliced

*baking tray, lined with
baking parchment*

METHOD

1. Preheat the oven to 180°C (160°C fan/350°F/Gas 4).

2. Season the chicken with salt and pepper. Put the beaten eggs in one bowl, the flour in another bowl and the breadcrumbs in a third bowl. Season the flour with salt, pepper, the turmeric and 1 tsp curry powder.

3. Dip the chicken into the flour, then the egg and then the breadcrumbs. Repeat the process if you need to, to ensure that the chicken is thoroughly coated. Put the chicken onto the lined baking tray, drizzle over the vegetable oil and bake for 25 minutes until cooked.

4. Pour the rice into a measuring jug to find its volume, then place in a saucepan with 1½ times the amount of water. Add a pinch of salt. Cover with a lid and simmer until all the water has gone. Leave to stand for 10 minutes with the lid on. Use a fork to fluff the grains.

5. For the sauce, heat the rapeseed oil in a pan over a medium heat, add the onion and carrot and cook for 4–5 minutes until soft but not coloured. Add the garlic, curry powder and garam masala and cook for another 2 minutes. Add the peanut butter and stock and simmer gently for 2 minutes, stirring to make sure the peanut butter has dissolved. Remove from the heat and blend to a smooth sauce with a stick blender.

6. Put the rice into small bowls and pack it down. Slice the chicken and add it to the bowls with the sauce, spring onions and chilli.

Serves 4 / Prep 10 minutes / Cook 25 minutes / 134 kcal, 6.4g fat, 13g carbs, 4.2g protein

Roasted Miso Aubergine

This dish can either be served as a side dish or served with salad leaves and a light dressing as a main course. Aubergines are a great alternative to meat. They absorb flavours really well and this recipe is even vegan-friendly. (Pictured, page 84–85.)

INGREDIENTS

2 large aubergines
8 tbsp miso paste
2 tsp caster sugar
2 tbsp mirin or rice
  vinegar (optional)
1 tbsp sesame oil
3cm (1¼in) piece fresh
  root ginger, grated
2 tbsp flaked almonds,
  toasted
a few fresh coriander
  leaves

*baking tray, lined with
  baking parchment*

METHOD

1. Preheat the oven to 180°C (160°C fan/350°F/Gas 4).

2. Cut the aubergines in half and score the skin in a diamond pattern, taking care not to cut all the way through. Place them on the lined baking tray.

3. Mix together the miso, sugar, mirin, oil and ginger. Spoon the mixture over the cut side of the aubergines and spread it out over the surface.

4. Bake the aubergines in the oven for 25 minutes until the flesh is soft and the surface is light golden brown. Sprinkle with the toasted almonds and coriander. Serve.

Serves 2 / Prep 15 minutes / Cook 5 minutes / 701 kcal, 37g fat, 64g carbs, 20g protein

Edamame Salad

Edamame used to be a bit of a pain to get hold of, let alone prep. However, most supermarkets now have them in the freezer aisle. You simply blanch them in boiling water and you are ready to go. Sprinkling them with a little chilli salt turns them into a great little snack, too.

INGREDIENTS

100g (3½oz) dried rice
  noodles
150g (5oz) frozen shelled
  edamame
½ cucumber, cut in half,
  deseeded and sliced
5 radishes, sliced
1 avocado, peeled, stone
  removed and diced
1 carrot, grated
1 red pepper, finely diced
small handful of salted
  peanuts or cashew nuts,
  roughly chopped
fresh coriander leaves

DRESSING

4 tbsp soy sauce
2 tbsp sesame oil
1 tsp chopped fresh red
  chilli
1 tbsp honey
juice of 1 lime
1 tbsp grated fresh root
  ginger

METHOD

1. Place all the dressing ingredients into a jam jar, seal and shake well.

2. Place the rice noodles in a shallow bowl and pour over boiling water until covered. Leave to stand for 5 minutes, then drain.

3. Cook the edamame according to the packet instructions, then drain and run under cold water.

4. Place the cooked and cooled edamame in a bowl and add the cucumber, radishes, avocado, carrot, pepper and drained noodles. Give everything a good mix, then add the dressing. Serve in bowls topped with chopped nuts and coriander.

Serves 2 / Prep 15 minutes / Cook 10 minutes / 636 kcal, 15g fat, 102g carbs, 18g protein

Yaki Udon Noodles

This is a delicious vegetable dish, that can be made totally vegan swapping the Worcestershire sauce and honey for a pinch of salt and maple syrup. And if you're not vegan, you can always add some sliced pork fillet, chicken or prawns if you want to add some more protein.

INGREDIENTS

1 tbsp sesame oil
1 red onion, finely sliced
¼ white cabbage, finely
  sliced
200g (7oz) mushrooms,
  sliced
1 carrot, grated
1 pepper (colour of your
  choice), very finely sliced
400g (14oz) cooked udon
  noodles
3 spring onions, sliced
1 tsp black or white
  sesame seeds
25g (¾oz) salted cashew
  nuts, chopped
pickled ginger, to serve
lime wedges, to serve

SAUCE

3 tbsp mirin
3 tbsp soy sauce
1 tbsp honey
1 tbsp Worcestershire
  sauce

METHOD

1. Mix together the sauce ingredients and set aside.

2. Heat the sesame oil in a wok, then add the onion and cabbage. Stir-fry for 2 minutes, then add the mushrooms, carrot and pepper. Stir-fry for a further 2 minutes, then add in the noodles and sauce. Stir-fry everything together until warmed through.

3. Sprinkle over the spring onions, sesame seeds and chopped cashew nuts, and serve with pickled ginger and lime wedges.

Serves 4 as a starter / Prep 10 minutes / Cook 10 minutes / 145 kcal, 3.7g fat, 5.0g carbs, 23g protein

Prawn Lollipops

These are a perfect little starter or they can easily be served as a nibble at a party. The prawn mixture sticks together really well, making them quite easy to prepare. (Pictured, page 84–85.)

INGREDIENTS

500g (1lb 2oz) raw peeled
  king prawns
small bunch of coriander,
  leaves picked
2 garlic cloves, grated
1 red chilli, chopped
5cm (2in) piece fresh root
  ginger, grated
1 tbsp vegetable oil

DIPPING SAUCE

2 tbsp sweet chilli sauce
grated zest and juice of
  1 lime
1 tsp finely chopped fresh
  red chilli
1 tbsp fish sauce
  (optional)

*baking tray, lined with
  baking parchment*

METHOD

1. Preheat the oven to 200°C (180°C fan/400°F/Gas 6).

2. Place the prawns, coriander leaves, garlic, red chilli and ginger in a small food processor. Blitz until a paste is made (it doesn't have to be completely smooth).

3. Tip the paste into a bowl, then, with slightly wet hands, roll the mix into balls and pop them on the lined baking tray.

4. Drizzle them with the oil, then pop them in the oven for 8–10 minutes or until pink and cooked through.

5. While the prawn balls are cooking, mix together the sauce ingredients.

6. When the prawn balls are cooked, take them out of the oven and place them on cocktail sticks or lollipop sticks ready to dip in the sauce.

PRESERVED LEMONS

الشرق الأوسط

Middle Eastern Kitchen

As you can tell, I love all food, but I have a favourite and that is the food from the Middle East. I love it. I was lucky enough to spend a reasonable amount of time in the Middle East as a flower, fruit and veg buyer when I was younger, and there is something about the region that I just fell in love with. The food was a big part of that.

Each country has its own style, but there are certain themes that run through the cuisines, whether it be Israeli, Arabic or Iranian food. All the dishes are delicately spiced and full of the good fats like olive oil, the nuttiness of sesame, the freshness of parsley and mint, and the natural sweetness of dates and honey.

I love communal eating and, for me, Middle Eastern cuisine is best served in the middle of the table for everyone to dive in: vegetables, salads, breads, dips and deliciously seasoned meat. Now, where's my passport?

Serves 4–6 / Prep 45 minutes / Cook 50 minutes / 590 kcal, 18g fat, 70g carbs, 25g protein

Healthier Falafel Feast

I love falafel in a wrap or pitta bread with some crispy fresh veg, some pickles and possibly a touch too much chilli sauce. These are baked not fried, so they are a little drier than some falafel, but when you eat them with hummus or tzatziki, you won't be able to tell.

INGREDIENTS

1 tsp olive oil
1 large white onion, finely
   chopped
2 x 400g cans chickpeas,
   drained rinsed
2 garlic cloves, crushed
2 carrots, grated and
   juices squeezed out
2 tsp ground cumin
2 tsp ground coriander
2 tsp sea salt
1 tsp ground black pepper
handful of chopped fresh
   coriander
handful of chopped flat
   leaf parsley
40g (1½oz) plain flour
grated zest and juice of
   1 lemon
low-calorie oil spray
hummus, see page 100
salt and pepper

METHOD

1. For the falafel, preheat the oven to 190°C (170°C fan/375°F/Gas 5).

2. Heat the olive oil in a small frying pan over a medium heat. Add the onion and cook for about 10 minutes, or until softened and starting to brown (add a splash of water if the onion starts to stick).

3. Remove from the heat and leave to cool. Put the onion, chickpeas, garlic, carrots, spices, salt, pepper, chopped herbs, flour and lemon zest and juice in a food processor. Pulse until the mixture is fairly smooth – you want to retain some texture, but the paste should be able to hold together.

4. Divide the mixture into 18 equal pieces and shape into patties. Place on a baking tray lined with baking parchment and spray the patties with 10 sprays of oil. Cook on the top shelf of the oven for 20–25 minutes, or until golden brown.

TZATZIKI

200ml (7fl oz) plain yogurt
140g (5oz) cucumber,
 grated
1 garlic clove, crushed or
 grated
2 tbsp finely chopped mint
pinch of sugar (optional)

CHILLI SAUCE

400g can chopped
 tomatoes
2 tbsp tomato ketchup
1 small onion, chopped
3 garlic cloves
2 red chillies
pinch of sugar
1 tbsp white wine vinegar

GARLIC SAUCE

2 tbsp plain yogurt
2 tbsp mayonnaise
grated zest of 1 lemon,
 plus the juice, if needed
1 whole bulb of garlic,
 roasted in foil for
 20–30 minutes

SALAD

¼ red cabbage, finely
 shredded
¼ white cabbage, finely
 shredded
2 carrots, grated
juice of ½ orange
2 handfuls of pomegranate
 seeds (I use frozen, just
 defrost before use)

5. For the tzatziki, put the yogurt into a small bowl. Squeeze the grated cucumber to remove any excess liquid and then add it to the yogurt with the garlic, mint, salt and a pinch of sugar, if you need it. Mix well and set aside.

6. For the chilli sauce, , simply put all the ingredients into a food processor and blitz up. If you don't have a food processor, just grate or finely chop all the ingredients and mix together.

7. For the garlic sauce, mix the yogurt, mayonnaise and lemon zest in a bowl. Take the whole bulb of garlic, cut the top off and squeeze all the roasted garlic into the mayo and yogurt mixture. Season with salt and pepper, adding a little squeeze of lemon, if it needs it.

8. For the salad, mix together the shredded cabbages and grated carrots. Squeeze over the orange juice and sprinkle over the pomegranate seeds. Mix together and lightly season. You don't really want this to have too much flavour – you want it to be a crisp, clean contrast to the other flavours.

9. Lower the oven to 180°C (160°C fan/350°F/Gas 4) and move the tray of falafel to the bottom shelf of the oven. Bake for a further 20–25 minutes, or until cooked through. Sprinkle with a little salt. Serve the falafels with the hummus, tzatziki, chilli sauce, garlic sauce and salad as a feast to share.

Salmon & Tabbouleh Salad

Tabbouleh is served everywhere in the Middle East – it is served at parties, at evening meals and even as fast food in the shopping malls. It's the equivalent of a standard salad of lettuce, tomato and cucumber in the UK, but with more flavour.

INGREDIENTS

2 tbsp harissa paste
2 garlic cloves, crushed
1 tsp ground cumin
grated zest and juice of
  1 lemon
4 skinless salmon fillets

TABBOULEH

150g (5oz) bulgur wheat
4 large ripe tomatoes,
  finely chopped
large bunch of flat leaf
  parsley, finely chopped
small bunch of mint,
  finely chopped
½ cucumber, deseeded
  and finely chopped
1 red onion, finely chopped
grated zest and juice of
  1 lemon
2 tbsp olive oil
salt and pepper

*baking tray, lined with
  baking parchment*

METHOD

1. Preheat the oven to 180°C (160°C fan/350°F/Gas 4).

2. In a large bowl, mix together the harissa paste, garlic, cumin and lemon zest and juice. Add the salmon and cover the fillets with the marinade. Leave to marinate for as long as you can, but at least 20 minutes.

3. Place the fillets onto the prepared baking tray and bake in the oven for 20 minutes.

4. Meanwhile, prepare the tabbouleh. Place the bulgur wheat in a bowl and cover with 100ml (3½fl oz) boiling water, stir, cover and leave to absorb for 20 minutes.

5. Place all the chopped ingredients with the lemon zest, juice and olive oil into another bowl, season and mix together.

6. When the bulgur wheat has absorbed the water, fluff it up with a fork and add to the herbs and tomatoes, along with the lemon zest and juice and olive oil. Mix together and season to taste further with salt and pepper, if needed.

★ Make it gluten-free by using quinoa instead of bulgur wheat!

Lamb Meatballs with a Crunchy Salad

INGREDIENTS

500g (1lb 2 oz) minced lamb
1 white onion and 1 large
  carrot, grated
3 garlic cloves, crushed
1 tsp each sea salt, ground
  black pepper, ground
  cumin, ground coriander
  and ground cinnamon
pinch of ground nutmeg
1 egg, beaten
1 tbsp olive oil

SALAD

2 tbsp plain yogurt
grated zest and juice of
  1 lemon
4 large carrots, grated
100g (3½oz) radishes and
  1 red onion, finely sliced
100g (3½oz) tomatoes and
  ½ cucumber, chopped
large bunch of parsley and
  handful of mint, chopped
2 handfuls of pistachio nuts,
  roughly chopped
2 handfuls of pomegranate
  seeds

*baking tray, lined with baking
  parchment*

METHOD

1. Preheat the oven to 180°C (160°C fan/350°F/Gas 4).

2. In a large bowl, mix together the minced lamb, onion, carrot and garlic. Add the salt, pepper, spices and egg and mix well. Now take a little of the mixture and roll into a smallish ball, smaller than a golf ball – you want to be able to make about 18–20 balls.

3. Heat the olive oil in a frying pan, then brown 5–6 meatballs at a time, in batches. When they have a good colour, transfer them to the lined baking tray and repeat with the rest.

4. Bake the meatballs in the oven for 15–20 minutes.

5. Meanwhile, prepare the salad. In a bowl, mix together the yogurt and lemon zest and juice and season well.

6. Mix together all the vegetables and herbs in another large bowl, then mix through the yogurt dressing. Sprinkle with the pistachio nuts and pomegranate seeds, and serve with the meatballs.

Serves 4 / Prep 15 minutes (plus marinating) / Cook 10–15 minutes / 215 kcal, 11g fat, 9.9g carbs, 17g protein

Minty Lamb Kebabs

The combination of lamb and mint is a marriage made in heaven, and this recipe is no exception. For extra sauces, hop over to the falafel feast on pages 90–91, where you will find classic garlic and chilli sauces.

INGREDIENTS

150ml (5fl oz) plain yogurt
2 tbsp mint sauce
1 tsp ground cumin
1 tsp ground coriander
1 red chilli, finely chopped
  or ½ tsp crushed dried
  chillies
300g (10½oz) diced lamb
1 white onion, cut into
  small chunks
1 red pepper, cut into
  small chunks

*kebab sticks (if wooden,
  please soak first)*

METHOD

1. Heat the grill to medium.

2. In a bowl, mix the yogurt and mint sauce together, then set aside a couple of tablespoons of the mint yogurt for a dip.

3. Into the rest of the mint yogurt, add the cumin, coriander and most of the red chilli (reserving a little for sprinkling over at the end).

4. Add the lamb into the yogurt mix and leave to marinate for at least 20 minutes, or overnight, if you can.

5. Now assemble the kebabs, alternating between lamb, onion and pepper. Be careful not to push them together too tightly, as that will prevent the heat being able to cook things evenly.

6. Put the kebabs under the grill and cook for 6–7 minutes on each side until cooked to your liking.

7. When finished, scatter with the remaining chilli. Serve with the reserved mint yogurt for dipping, plus wraps or pitta breads and whatever salad you fancy.

Serves 4 / Prep 25 minutes / Cook 30 minutes / 590 kcal, 32g fat, 50g carbs, 20g protein

Hummus & Roasted Squash Wraps

Shop-bought hummus is very high in fat and salt. Making it yourself is super-quick if you have a blender, and it will have less than half the fat and salt. Make a big batch and store it in an airtight container in the fridge for up to 3 days.

INGREDIENTS

400g can chickpeas,
  drained and rinsed
2 tbsp tahini
1 large garlic clove
3 tbsp olive oil
juice of ½ lemon
salt

SQUASH

350g (12oz) butternut
  squash, peeled and diced
1 tbsp olive oil
1 tsp smoked hot paprika

TO SERVE

4 flour tortilla wraps
150g (5½oz) jarred
  roasted red peppers,
  drained and cut into
  strips
large handful of rocket
a little feta cheese
1 tbsp sunflower seeds

METHOD

1. Place the chickpeas and tahini in a food processor along with the garlic and start to blitz. Pour in the olive oil and blend again until smooth. Add the lemon juice to taste and, if it is a little thick, add a little splash of water. Season with salt.

2. Preheat the oven to 190°C (170°C fan/375°F/Gas 5).

3. For the squash, spread out the diced butternut squash on a baking tray lined with baking parchment. Drizzle with the oil, sprinkle over the paprika and a pinch of salt, and toss together, then spread it out again. Roast in the oven for 25–30 minutes until tender.

4. Spread a big spoonful of the hummus on each tortilla. Top with some of the roasted butternut squash and strips of roasted pepper. Add some rocket, crumble over a little feta and sprinkle over some seeds. Fold the bottom of the wrap over to stop the filling falling out, then roll the wrap up and serve.

Serves 4 / Prep 20 minutes / Cook 25 minutes / 404 kcal, 15g fat, 44g carbs, 19g protein

Chicken Tagine Soup

I love this soup, it's exactly what a soup should be. Healthy and hearty, with a bit of spice, too. If you don't have any pearl barley, you can always add chickpeas instead and reduce the amount of stock by a quarter, but the barley turns this into a one-pot-wonder of a meal.

INGREDIENTS

2 tbsp olive oil
1 onion, chopped
2 celery sticks, finely chopped
1 large carrot, finely chopped
2 garlic cloves, grated
3 tsp harrisa paste or harrisa spice blend
1 tbsp tomato purée
2 x 400g cans chopped tomatoes
1 litre (1¾ pints) chicken stock
150g (5oz) pearl barley, rinsed
small handful of raisins
150g (5oz) cooked roast chicken, cut into bite-sized pieces
handful of fresh parsley and coriander, chopped
salt and pepper
4 tbsp crème fraîche

METHOD

1. Heat the olive oil in a large saucepan. Add the onion, celery and carrot and cook on a medium-low heat for 5 minutes.

2. Add the garlic, harrisa and tomato purée and stir for 1 minute before pouring in the tomatoes, stock and pearl barley. Bring the soup to the boil and simmer for 20 minutes.

3. After 20 minutes, stir in the raisins and chicken and simmer gently for a further 5 minutes to warm through. (If you are using raw chicken, add this with the pearl barley.) Once the chicken is warmed through and the barley is tender, stir in half of the chopped herbs and season with salt and pepper.

4. Spoon into bowls and top each portion with a dollop of crème fraîche, then sprinkle over the rest of the chopped herbs.

Serves 4–6 / Prep 10 minutes / Cook 50 minutes / 277 kcal, 7.7g fat, 22g carbs, 27g protein

Chicken &
Chickpea Stew

Stews don't have to be cooked on the hob; they can easily be cooked in the oven where you don't have to keep an eye on them too closely. This is a perfect throw-it-in-the-dish, throw-it-in-the-oven kind of meal.

INGREDIENTS

1 tbsp olive oil or low-calorie oil spray
4–6 skinless, boneless chicken thighs
400g can chickpeas, drained and rinsed
400g can chopped tomatoes
3 garlic cloves, crushed
2 red onions, finely chopped
1 yellow pepper, finely sliced
grated zest and juice of 1 lemon
1 tbsp ras el hanout (if you can't get this, mix 1 tsp each of ground coriander, ground cumin and ground cinnamon, plus a pinch of ground nutmeg)
salt
handful of flat leaf parsley, chopped

METHOD

1. Preheat the oven to 180°C (160°C fan/350°F/Gas 4).

2. Drizzle the oil onto a baking tray or spray the tray with low-calorie spray. Add the chicken thighs, pour in the chickpeas and tomatoes, then add all the other ingredients, except the salt and parsley and mix well. Once well mixed, spread everything out evenly in the baking tray.

3. Cook in the oven for 50 minutes, or until the chicken is cooked through (if you need to leave it in for another 5–10 minutes, then please do).

4. Season with salt, then sprinkle over the chopped parsley and serve.

Feta, Fig & Beetroot Salad

Vac-pac cooked beetroot is a great quick-to-use ingredient, but if you have the time or a glut of beetroot from the garden, then simply roast the beets in the oven for 1 hour and then rub off the skins. Try to get hold of candy and golden beetroot to make this dish look extra-special.

INGREDIENTS

500g (1lb 2oz) cooked
  beetroot, sliced
6–8 fresh figs, cut into
  quarters (if not in
  season, use pears)
2 tbsp honey
100g (3½oz) baby spinach
  leaves
100g (3½oz) rocket
400g (14oz) feta cheese,
  crumbled
1 red onion, finely sliced
3 tbsp olive oil
grated zest and juice of
  1 lemon
1 tbsp Dijon or wholegrain
  mustard
2 handfuls of walnuts,
  crushed

METHOD

1. Preheat the oven to 150°C (130°C fan/300°F/Gas 2).

2. Place the beetroot and the figs on a baking tray, drizzle with the honey and cook in the oven for 10 minutes.

3. Place the spinach and rocket in a serving dish, then layer on the beetroot, figs, feta and red onion.

4. To make the dressing, place the olive oil, lemon zest and juice and mustard into a jar, seal and shake well. Drizzle the dressing over the salad, and add the crushed walnuts before serving.

Serves 2 / Prep 10 minutes / Cook 25 minutes / 494 kcal, 20g fat, 51g carbs, 23g protein

Shakshuka

Shakshuka is traditionally a breakfast or brunch dish from North Africa, but I've adapted this for a perfect lunch or dinner dish. Served on flatbreads, so it resembles a pizza, it is the perfect, quick family meal.

INGREDIENTS

1 tbsp vegetable oil
1 onion, sliced
1 pepper, sliced
1 garlic clove, crushed
1 tsp ground cumin
½ tsp smoked paprika
½ tsp chopped fresh chilli
 or crushed dried chillies
400g can chopped
 tomatoes
200g (7oz) baby spinach
 leaves
salt and pepper
2 large flatbreads (thicker
 ones are better than the
 thinner ones)
2 eggs
handful of fresh
 coriander
50g (1¾ oz) feta cheese or
 grated cheese

METHOD

1. Heat the oil in a frying pan and add the onion and pepper. Cook for 2 minutes, then stir in the garlic, cumin, paprika and chilli. Cook for 1 minute, then stir in the tomatoes. Simmer gently for 10 minutes, or until reduced and thickened, stirring every now and then.

2. Stir in the spinach and allow it to wilt, then simmer for a further couple of minutes to remove the excess water from the spinach. Season with salt and pepper.

3. Meanwhile, preheat the oven to 180°C (160°C fan/350°F/Gas 4).

4. Place the flatbreads on a baking tray, divide the shakshuka mixture between them and spread it out, leaving a little border around the edge. Make a well in the centre of each portion of sauce, then crack an egg into each one. Bake them in the oven for 12 minutes or until the egg white is cooked.

5. Sprinkle over the coriander and feta, then serve.

Serves 4 / Prep 15 minutes (plus resting) / Cook 15 minutes / 593 kcal, 13g fat, 75g carbs, 41g protein

Turkish Pizza

These delicious pizza-like-breads are a staple snack in Turkey. Traditionally, they are pinched in at the ends to make a boat shape, and often filled with minced lamb or beef.

INGREDIENTS

350g (12oz) strong white flour
1 tsp fine salt
1 tsp caster sugar
150ml (5fl oz) milk
4g (⅛ oz) fast-action dried yeast

TOPPING

1 tbsp olive oil
400g (14oz) minced beef
2 garlic cloves, crushed
1 tsp ground cumin
1 tsp ground coriander
½ tsp ground cinnamon
2 tbsp tomato purée
300g (10½oz) spinach
50g (1¾oz) feta cheese
4 spring onions, sliced
sumac, to taste

YOGURT DIP

4 tbsp plain yogurt
1 garlic clove, crushed
1 tbsp chopped fresh coriander
grated zest of 1 lemon
handful of mint leaves

METHOD

1. Place the flour in a large bowl, then add the salt and sugar. Warm the milk in a small pan, just to take the chill off it, then add the yeast (the milk must only be warm, not boiling). Pour the milk mixture into the flour and use the end of a wooden spoon to start to mix it together. Once you have a ball of dough, knead it on a lightly floured surface until smooth and elastic.

2. Place the dough back into a clean bowl, cover and leave it to rise for 1 hour, or until it has doubled in size.

3. Meanwhile, heat the oil in a frying pan, then crumble in the beef. Fry until the meat is browned, then add the garlic and spices. Cook for a further minute, then stir in the tomato purée. Cook for 2 minutes, then add the spinach and cook until wilted. Season well with salt.

4. Preheat the oven to 200°C (180°C fan/400°F/Gas 6).

5. Take the dough from the bowl and knead it a few times to get rid of any air. Roll the dough out into an oval shape, then top with the meat mixture, leaving a 2cm (¾in) border all the way around the edge.

6. Fold the border in over the topping and pinch the ends to make a boat shape. Sprinkle with the feta cheese, spring onions and sumac. Bake in the oven for 10 minutes.

7. Mix together the yogurt, garlic, coriander, lemon zest and a pinch of salt. Remove the pizza from the oven and serve with fresh mint scattered over and the yogurt dip.

Rosewater Lemonade

INGREDIENTS

juice of 7 lemons
4 tbsp honey
1.5 litres (2¾ pints) sparkling water
½ tsp rosewater
ice cubes, to serve

METHOD

1. Mix everything together, then serve.

Pomegranate Punch

INGREDIENTS

1 litre (1¾ pints) pomegranate juice
500ml (16fl oz) ginger ale
juice of 4 limes
ice cubes, to serve

METHOD

1. Mix everything together, then serve.

Mint Lemonade

INGREDIENTS

juice of 10 lemons
large bunch of mint, leaves picked
60g (2oz) caster sugar
1 litre (1¾ pints) sparkling water
ice cubes, to serve

METHOD

1. Blend the lemon juice, mint and sugar with a little water until the mint is very finely chopped. Pour into a jug, then top up with sparkling water and serve with ice cubes.

Pizzeria

I love Italian food. There is something quite simple, but magical about it. For me, Italian food is about letting the ingredients do the talking, and once you have mastered the tomato sauce or pesto, you will never go hungry again. Very easy, very cheap, but very delicious, and, with lots of these things, you can make a big batch and freeze it!

Italian food is one of the cuisines we have not only taken to our hearts, but really welcomed into our homes. Although there are some foods we still shy away from cooking from scratch, and one of those is probably the most famous Italian export, pizza!

Little mopeds are dropping off these delicious pizzas up and down the country, all day and into the night. Undeniably delicious, but big on calories and price, especially when you consider the ingredients are very inexpensive. You can easily make your own and save your self a fortune and lots of calories. There are loads of family favourites in this chapter and hopefully a few new ones...

Serves 4 / Prep 15 minutes / Cook 30 minutes / 504 kcal, 15g fat, 74g carbs, 16g protein

Quick-&-Easy Flatbread Pizza

Sometimes, when we are in a rush, we cheat and use shop-bought flatbreads and let the kids add their own toppings, which they love. My eldest son isn't a great fan of pizza, but he enjoys making them with flatbreads! You can add some dried herbs to the dough, if you like.

INGREDIENTS

350g (12oz) plain flour, plus extra for dusting
salt and freshly ground black pepper
3 tbsp olive oil, plus extra for greasing
150ml (5fl oz) warm water
2 garlic cloves, crushed
400-g can cherry tomatoes
large handful of grated mozzarella
½ red onion, finely sliced
toppings of your choice, such as sliced red onion, sliced mushrooms, tinned sweetcorn, sliced courgettes, sliced peppers, black olives or even pineapple, if that's your thing!

2 baking trays, lined with baking parchment

METHOD

1. For the flatbreads, sift the flour into a large mixing bowl and season with salt and pepper. Create a little well in the middle of the flour and add 2 tbsp of the olive oil, then start to add the water and mix well until you have a thick, but not too sticky, dough.

2. Knead the dough on a floured work surface for 1 minute or until smooth, then put the dough in a lightly oiled bowl, cover and rest for 10 minutes.

3. For the pizza sauce, heat the remaining 1 tbsp olive oil and gently heat the garlic for a minute, taking care not to burn it. Add the can of cherry tomatoes and heat for 3–4 minutes. Using a potato masher, squash the tomatoes – you don't want to make it totally smooth, just start breaking the tomatoes a bit. Leave on a gentle heat for 10 minutes until it reduces down a sauce that is thick enough to spread on your flatbread.

4. Preheat the oven to 220°C (200°C fan/425°F/Gas 7).

5. Divide the dough into four balls and roll each one out to a thin pizza base. Put them on the lined baking trays and cook in the hot oven for 2 minutes. Remove the trays from the oven and turn the flatbreads over.

6. Spread the tomato sauce over the cooked sides of the pizzas, sprinkle over the grated mozzarella and then top with your veggies. Pop them back in the oven for 7–8 minutes or until the cheese is all melted.

Makes 4 / Prep 20 minutes / Cook 30 minutes / 564 kcal, 36g fat, 16g carbs, 39g protein

Cauliflower Pizza

GF

INGREDIENTS

1 cauliflower, about 800g
  (1¾lb)
150g (5½oz) ground
  almonds
2 eggs, beaten
2 tsp chopped fresh
  parsley
50g (1¾oz) finely grated
  Parmesan
salt and pepper

TOPPING

2 tbsp tomato purée
2 tomatoes, sliced
a few mushrooms, thinly
  sliced
1 courgette
½ red onion, thinly sliced
2 x 125g (4½oz) balls
  mozzarella, drained well
4 slices Parma ham
handful of fresh basil

*baking tray, lined with
  baking parchment*

METHOD

1. Cut the cauliflower into quarters. Place two quarters into a food processor and blitz until finely chopped. Transfer to a heatproof bowl and repeat with the remaining quarters.

2. Cover the bowl with clingfilm and microwave on high for 6 minutes. Leave to stand for 5 minutes, before tipping it out onto a clean tea towel to cool.

3. Preheat the oven to 190°C (170°C fan/375°F/Gas 5).

4. Tip it back into the bowl and stir in the almonds, eggs, parsley and Parmesan. Season well and mix together.

5. Spoon the cauliflower mix into four piles on the lined baking tray. Spread each one out to create a 12–15cm (5–6in) circle. Bake in the oven for 16–18 minutes or until starting to go crispy around the edge.

6. Remove from the oven and leave to cool slightly. Turn the oven up to 220°C (200°C fan/425°F/Gas 7).

7. For the topping, season the tomato purée with salt and pepper, then spread it out over the four pizza bases. Place a few slices of tomato on top of the purée, then add a few mushroom slices. Use a vegetable peeler to make ribbons of courgette, and place those on top with the sliced red onion. Tear over the mozzarella.

8. Bake in the oven for 12 minutes, then remove from the oven and top with the Parma ham and fresh basil leaves. Serve with salad leaves.

Makes 4 / Prep 40 minutes / Cook 15 minutes / 409 kcal, 13g fat, 55g carbs, 17g protein

Calzone

The calzone is Italy's answer to the Cornish pasty. Street venders are found all over Italy selling these as the pizza that you can walk and talk with. Watch out: the first bite will be HOT!

INGREDIENTS

250g (9oz) strong white flour, plus extra for dusting
5g (⅛oz) fast-action dried yeast
a pinch of caster sugar
¾ tsp salt
150ml (5fl oz) warm water
2 tbsp extra-virgin olive oil
200g (7oz) cherry tomatoes
1 tbsp olive oil
1 red onion, finely chopped
1 red pepper, finely chopped
100g (3½oz) mushrooms, chopped
1 courgette, chopped
salt and pepper
3 tbsp tomato purée
125g ball mozzarella, torn

2 baking trays, lined with baking parchment

METHOD

1. Place the flour in a large bowl. Add the yeast and sugar to one side of the bowl and the salt to the other side. Pour in the warm water and extra-virgin olive oil and start mixing the dough with the end of a wooden spoon until it comes together. You may need more water.

2. Tip it out onto a lightly floured work surface. Knead for 5 minutes until smooth and elastic. Place in a lightly oiled bowl, cover with clingfilm and leave in a warm place for 30–60 minutes, or until doubled in size.

3. Punch the air out of the dough and knead a couple of times. Divide the dough into four pieces and roll each out into a 25cm (10in) circle.

4. Preheat the oven to 220°C (200°C fan/425°F/Gas 7).

5. Quarter the tomatoes. Heat the olive oil in a pan and soften the onion for 5 minutes. Add the pepper and tomatoes and cook for 1 minute. Stir in the mushrooms and courgette and cook for 2 minutes. Season well.

6. Spread the tomato purée onto the dough bases, leaving a 2cm (¾in) gap around the edge. Top with a couple of spoonfuls of the veg mixture and some mozzarella. Brush the edge of the dough with a little water, then fold the dough in half, and press the edges together. Fold the edges back onto themselves, creating a lip. Place the calzones on the lined baking trays. Bake in the oven for 15 minutes.

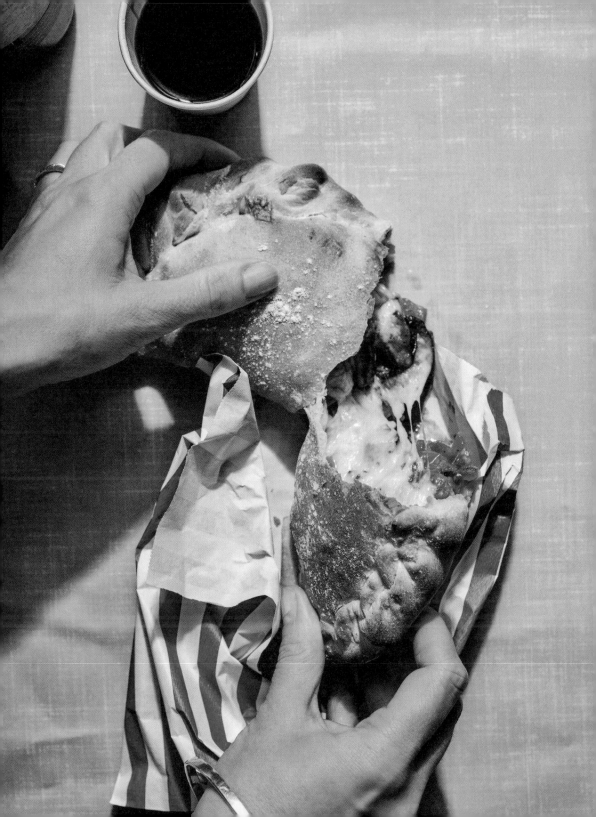

Serves 4 / Prep 15 minutes / Cook 20 minutes / 584 kcal, 18g fat, 71g carbs, 31g protein

Healthier Carbonara

Any Italian reading this will be going mad. Carbonara is not to be messed with in Italy, so adding peas or any other veg is a no-no! It will always be an indulgent dish with all that cheese, so adding a little veg can't hurt, can it?

INGREDIENTS

350g (12oz) dried
  spaghetti
salt and pepper
1 tbsp olive oil
85g (3oz) bacon or
  pancetta, chopped into
  small strips
2–3 garlic cloves,
  crushed or finely
  chopped
200g (7oz) frozen peas,
  defrosted
3 eggs, beaten
100g (3½oz) Parmesan,
  grated, plus (optional)
  extra to serve

METHOD

1. Cook the spaghetti in a large pan of boiling salted water for about 8 minutes, then check it – you want it to have a fraction more bite than you would usually, as you will cook it a little longer later. We want it just a little al dente at this stage.

2. Heat the oil in the largest frying pan you have and fry the bacon or pancetta for 5 minutes until it starts to go crispy. Now stir in the garlic and cook for another 2 minutes, then tip in the defrosted peas.

3. Don't drain the spaghetti, but use tongs to take it from the water into the frying pan with the bacon and the garlic (we are doing this as we will use some of the pasta water, so keep the pan of water to hand).

4. Once you have added the spaghetti to the frying pan with the garlic and bacon, mix everything together, then turn the heat off. Mix the beaten eggs and cheese together in a bowl.

5. Pour the eggs and cheese into the pan and mix well (the residual heat in the pan will be enough to gently heat the eggs and cheese). Add some of the pasta cooking water to loosen the sauce. Season well with pepper (you probably won't need salt) and finish with a bit more Parmesan to serve, if you would like.

Quick-&-Easy Tomato Sauce

This is so easy that you will never go back to a jar of ready-made sauce. This sauce (or variations of it) are the basis for so many different meals: Bolognese, lasagne, simple pasta, pizza.

INGREDIENTS

1 tbsp olive oil or low-calorie oil spray
2 onions, finely chopped
2 garlic cloves, crushed
1½ tbsp tomato purée
2 tbsp red wine (optional)
2 x 400g cans plum tomatoes
bunch of basil, torn
salt and pepper

METHOD

1. Heat the oil in a pan, add the onions and soften for 5 minutes, but don't let them take on any colour – add a splash of water to stop burning, if needed. Add the garlic, tomato purée and red wine, if using, and cook for 5 minutes more.

2. Pour in the tomatoes and simmer gently for 20 minutes. If using plum tomatoes, gently break them down during cooking.

3. Stir in the fresh basil and season generously with salt and pepper, then serve (or cool and freeze).

Red Pesto

My 7-year-old loves this on his pasta, so I always make a bigger batch and keep it in a sealed jar in the fridge for up to a week. There is no way Leo would eat a sun-dried tomato whole, but he loves this!

INGREDIENTS

200g (7oz) sun-dried tomatoes
handful of pitted black olives (optional)
2 tbsp roasted red peppers from a jar
4 garlic cloves
juice of ½ lemon
½ tsp sea salt
½ tsp freshly ground black pepper
1 tbsp olive oil
100g (3½oz) pine nuts

METHOD

1. Put all the ingredients into a blender or a food processor and blitz. This can be kept for up to a week in an airtight container in the fridge, or you can freeze it.

Serves 2–4 / Prep 10 minutes / Cook 5 minutes / 469 kcal, 34g fat, 19g carbs, 17g protein

Caesar Salad

Everybody knows that salads are good for you, until you load them with dressing, that is. However, this is a lighter version with a yogurt-based dressing – and if you are really watching your waistline, remember to use low-fat yogurt.

INGREDIENTS

3 tbsp olive oil
a few slices stale crusty
  bread
3 garlic cloves, crushed
grated zest of 1 lemon
  and juice of ½ lemon
30g (1oz) Parmesan,
  finely grated, plus extra
  to serve
3 anchovy fillets in oil,
  drained and finely
  chopped
1 tbsp white wine vinegar
1 tsp Worcestershire
  sauce
4 tbsp Greek yogurt
1 tsp English mustard
salt and pepper
2 Little Gem lettuces or
  1 large Romaine lettuce,
  thickly shredded
1 red onion, thinly sliced
½ cucumber, sliced
1 avocado, peeled, stone
  removed and diced
handful of green beans,
  blanched

METHOD

1. In a pan, gently heat 1 tbsp of the oil. Tear the bread into 1–2cm (½–¾in) cubes, then add the bread and 2 crushed garlic cloves to the oil in the pan. Toast it all in the oil until golden brown, turning occasionally then set aside.

2. In a jar or bowl, put the lemon zest and juice, Parmesan and the finely chopped anchovies. Add the white wine vinegar, remaining 2 tbsp olive oil, remaining 1 crushed garlic clove, the Worcestershire sauce, yogurt and mustard. Mix well, taste and season.

3. Toss the lettuce, onion, cucumber, avocado and green beans together in a bowl, mix the dressing through and top with the garlic croutons. Feel free to grate a little extra Parmesan over the top, too, if you like.

Serves 4–5 / Prep 30 minutes / Cook 18 minutes / 588 kcal, 32g fat, 62g carbs, 11g protein

Dough Balls & Garlic Butter

There is a well-known high street pizza chain that is almost as famous for their dough balls as they are for their pizza. These make a great starter or are a perfect way to use up some pizza dough. My kids like to make mini sandwiches for picnics with them, too.

INGREDIENTS

325g (11oz) strong white
  flour
7g (⅛oz) sachet fast-
  action dried yeast
2 tbsp olive oil, plus extra
  for greasing
2 tsp salt
250ml (9fl oz) warm water

GARLIC BUTTER

125g (4½oz) butter,
  softened
3 garlic cloves, crushed
sea salt
handful of flat leaf
  parsley, finely chopped
  (optional)

baking tray, greased

METHOD

1. Place the flour in a large mixing bowl, then add the yeast to one side of the bowl and the olive oil and salt to the other side of the bowl. Stir in the warm water, a little bit at a time, until a soft dough is formed. Turn it out onto a lightly floured work surface and knead for 5 minutes until smooth and elastic.

2. Place the dough in a lightly oiled bowl and cover with clingfilm. Leave in a warm place for 30–60 minutes, or until it has doubled in size.

3. Meanwhile, mix the butter, garlic, salt to taste and parsley in a small bowl until well combined. Keep as a firm butter for dipping your dough balls into or melt the garlic butter for brushing over the dough balls.

4. Once your dough has doubled in size, punch the air out of the dough. On a lightly floured surface, knead it a couple of times. Divide into 20 balls, each roughly the size of a 50p coin. Place the dough balls onto the greased baking tray. Cover with clingfilm and leave to prove in a warm place for 30 minutes.

5. Preheat the oven to 220°C (200°C fan/425°F/Gas 7).

6. Bake the dough balls for 15–18 minutes until risen and golden brown. Serve hot.

★ You can make double the garlic butter, roll it into a log, wrap it and freeze it for up to 1 month.

Taqueria

Mexican and Tex-Mex food is great fun. Wonderful platters of spicy nachos, chilli con carne or quesadillas are all full of flavour, colour and fun. I love this fusion food and so do my kids. The spicy, rich, smokey flavours always make me feel like it's a party.

Tex-Mex makes for a great night in with friends. The dips and salsas can all be made in advance, ready to be served later on; big pots of chilli or trays full of hot nachos with melting cheese are easy to make on a grand scale; and don't forget your guests do half the work for you when it comes to fajitas. *La cucaracha* anyone?

Dips & Chips

These quick dips and chips will take things to the next level when you've got friends round, and, best of all, the chips are oven-baked rather than fried – so tuck in!

INGREDIENTS

6 tortilla wraps
olive oil
salt and pepper

SALSA

4 large tomatoes
1 red onion, sliced
1 jalapeño chilli
a pinch of sugar (optional)

GUACAMOLE

2 avocados, peeled,
  halved and stones
  removed
½ small red onion, finely
  chopped
juice of 1–2 limes
1 tbsp chopped fresh
  coriander

CHIVE SOUR CREAM

1 small garlic clove
150ml (5fl oz) sour cream
1 tbsp snipped chives

METHOD

1. Preheat the oven to 180°C (160°C fan/350°F/Gas 4).

2. For the salsa, place the tomatoes, onion and chilli on a baking tray and drizzle with olive oil. Season with salt and pepper. Roast in the oven for 20 minutes, then leave to cool slightly. Leave the oven on for the tortilla chips.

3. Brush the tortilla wraps with oil on both sides, then cut them into triangles and place them on a couple of baking trays and sprinkle with salt. Bake them in the oven for 6–8 minutes, turning over halfway through, until golden brown and crisp. Leave to cool and, once cold, store in an airtight container.

4. For the guacamole, mash the avocado flesh, then stir in the onion, lime juice and coriander. Season with salt.

5. Take the roasted tomatoes and squeeze out some of the seeds. Place the tomatoes, onion and chilli in a blender. Pulse until the mixture is chopped but not smooth. Season with salt and a pinch of sugar, if needed.

6. For the chive sour cream, grate the garlic into the sour cream. Add the chives and season with salt and pepper.

7. Serve the homemade tortilla chips with the spicy salsa, guacamole and sour cream dips.

★ If you are feeling like a real treat, sprinkle some grated cheese over the tortilla chips and warm them in the oven before dunking.

Serves 4 / Prep 15 minutes / Cook 5 minutes . 656 kcal, 27g fat, 75g carbs, 24g protein

Prawn Tacos

Soft tortillas, filled with spicy prawns and topped with bright pink cabbage, are not only great fun to make, but they are also quick to cook. Good-quality prawns will have a sweet flavour.

INGREDIENTS

½ red cabbage, finely shredded
juice of 3 limes
1 tbsp caster sugar
salt
1 tbsp vegetable oil
1 garlic clove, sliced
1 tsp smoked paprika
300g (10½oz) raw king prawns, peeled and cleaned
100ml (3½fl oz) mayonnaise
2–3 tbsp chilli sauce
8 flour tortilla wraps, warmed
1 large avocado, peeled, stone removed and sliced
handful of chopped fresh coriander

METHOD

1. Place the cabbage in a bowl. Add the juice of 2 limes, the sugar and a pinch of salt. Mix well and leave to stand while you make the rest of the dish.

2. Mix together the oil, garlic and paprika in a bowl, then add the prawns and toss to mix. Set aside.

3. Mix together the mayonnaise and chilli sauce in a separate small bowl.

4. Heat a frying pan over a medium heat. Add the prawns and fry for 3–4 minutes until pink all over.

5. Drain the cabbage.

6. Spread a little of the spiced mayonnaise on each tortilla wrap and sprinkle over some of the pickled cabbage. Top with some cooked prawns, a few slices of avocado and some fresh coriander. Add an extra squeeze of lime, fold in half and enjoy!

★ Make fish tacos. Instead of the prawns, use 400g (14oz) cod fillet, cut into bite-sized pieces. Cook the cod, skin-side down first, for 3–4 minutes, turning once, until cooked through. Then continue as per the rest of the recipe.

Serves 4 / Prep 20 minutes / Cook 20 minutes / 513 kcal, 29g fat, 32g carbs, 27g protein

Loaded Nachos

This is ideal Friday-night chill-out food, perfect to share with friends and enjoy with a beer around the table. Make a double or triple batch of the meat and pop it in the freezer, then half the cooking is already done for another night when your mates turn up at the door.

INGREDIENTS

1 onion, finely chopped
1 red or green pepper, finely diced
1 tbsp olive oil
400g (14oz) minced beef
1 tsp smoked paprika
1 tsp ground cumin
½ tsp crushed dried chillies or chopped fresh chilli
200g (7oz) mushrooms, chopped
200g can chopped tomatoes
400g can kidney or pinto beans, drained and rinsed
1 tbsp chilli sauce
salt
170g (6oz) corn tortilla chips
100g (3½oz) grated cheese
1 avocado, peeled, stone removed and diced
150ml (5fl oz) sour cream

METHOD

1. First, make the meat sauce. Fry the onion and pepper in the oil for 3 minutes until soft. Add the beef, using a wooden spoon to break it up. Fry until browned all over.

2. Stir in the spices and chilli and fry for 30 seconds, then stir in the mushrooms and canned tomatoes. Cook for 1 minute, then add the beans and chilli sauce. Cook for 5 minutes. Season with salt. Remove from the heat.

3. To make the salsa, chop all the vegetables to the same size, then mix together in a bowl. Squeeze in the lime juice, season with salt and add some chopped coriander. Stir well.

4. Preheat the oven to 180°C (160°C fan/350°F/Gas 4).

5. Place half of the tortilla chips in a shallow ovenproof dish, top with half of the beef mixture and sprinkle over half of the cheese. Repeat with the remaining tortilla chips, beef and cheese. Bake in the oven for 8–10 minutes or until the cheese has just melted.

6. Remove from the oven and scatter with the diced avocado and salsa, add some sour cream, then tuck in!

SALSA

1 small red onion
6 tomatoes
½ chilli
juice of 1 lime
small bunch of fresh
  coriander
salt

Serves 4 / Prep 15 minutes / Cook 10 minutes / 608 kcal, 21g fat, 79g carbs, 21g protein

Refried Bean Quesadillas

I think we should all be eating a little less meat and tucking into veggies and pulses instead. This is a great meat-free option and can easily be made vegan by using vegan cheese and ditching the sour cream for a bit of guacamole.

INGREDIENTS

1 onion, chopped
2 garlic cloves, chopped
1 tbsp vegetable oil
½ tsp ground cumin
2 tsp smoked paprika
400g can kidney or pinto
  beans, drained
salt and pepper
8 flour tortilla wraps
4 spring onions, chopped
25g (1oz) feta cheese,
  crumbled
50g (1¾oz) grated cheese
sour cream, to serve

SALSA

2 tsp olive oil
200g (7oz) cherry
  tomatoes, cut into
  quarters
1 garlic clove, chopped
1 tsp white wine vinegar
1 tbsp sweet chilli sauce

METHOD

1. Start by making the salsa. Heat a small frying pan over a high heat. Add the oil, then the tomatoes and garlic, and fry for 30 seconds just to warm them through. Add the vinegar and allow it to bubble away before turning down the heat and adding the chilli sauce. Season with salt then set aside.

2. To make the quesadilla, fry the onion and garlic in the oil in a pan for 2 minutes, then stir in the cumin and paprika. Cook for 30 seconds, then add the beans with 2 tbsp of water. Warm the beans through, then use a masher or fork to smash the beans up until they are all broken. If they become too dry, add a little more water. Season well with salt and pepper.

3. Place four of the tortilla wraps on a board and divide the bean mixture between them. Spread the mixture out evenly, then sprinkle with chopped spring onions, crumbled feta and grated cheese. Place another tortilla on top of each one to make a sandwich.

4. Heat a large frying pan over a medium heat. Add one quesadilla to the pan and cook for 1 minute on each side or until golden brown. Remove from the pan and repeat with the remaining quesadillas.

5. Cut into quarters and serve with the tomato salsa and some sour cream.

Serves 4 / Prep 15 minutes / Cook 10 minutes / 848 kcal, 34g fat, 75g carbs, 54g protein

Quick-&-Easy Fajitas

Sometimes, when time is short, I want a great fajita, but with a few shortcuts. In this recipe, I make the salsa in the pan with the chicken by adding cherry tomatoes. Then some simple slices of avocado and a spritz of lime replaces the guacamole.

INGREDIENTS

2 tbsp olive oil
2 onions, sliced
2 red peppers, sliced
4 chicken breasts, thinly sliced
100g (3½oz) baby corn, halved
1 tsp chopped fresh red chilli
2 tsp smoked paprika
1 tsp ground coriander
200g (7oz) cherry tomatoes, halved
1 tbsp sweet chilli sauce (optional)
salt
large handful of chopped fresh coriander
8 tortilla wraps
100ml (3½oz) sour cream
50g (1¾oz) grated cheese
2 small avocados, peeled, stones removed and sliced
lime wedges, to serve

METHOD

1. Heat the oil in a large frying pan. Fry the onions and peppers for 3 minutes until slightly softened, then add the chicken, baby corn, chilli, smoked paprika and ground coriander. Stir well and cook for 2 minutes before adding the cherry tomatoes with 1 tbsp water.

2. Cook everything together on a medium heat, allowing the tomatoes to break up. Add the chilli sauce, if using, and cook for 2–3 minutes until the chicken is cooked through. Season with a little salt and stir in the fresh coriander.

3. Warm the tortilla wraps in the microwave or oven (according to the packet instructions) and pile them up with the chicken and veg mixture, sour cream, grated cheese and avocado slices. Serve with lime wedges for squeezing over.

Makes 12 / Prep 10 minutes / Cook 20 minutes / 108 kcal, 5.2g fat, 11g carbs, 4.0g protein

Sweetcorn Fritters

This is one of my go-to brunch recipes. The kids love them and they are packed full of veggies. If I'm being really indulgent, I add a couple of crispy rashers of bacon on top for good measure.

INGREDIENTS

100g (3½oz) plain flour
1 tsp smoked paprika
½ tsp baking powder
2 tbsp milk
3 eggs, beaten
300g (10½oz) canned or
  frozen sweetcorn,
  defrosted if frozen
4 spring onions, finely
  chopped
1 courgette, grated
1 tsp chopped fresh chilli
2 tbsp chopped fresh
  coriander
salt
olive oil or low-calorie oil
  spray
rocket leaves, to serve

HOT CRÈME FRAÎCHE

4 tbsp crème fraîche
2 tbsp sweet chilli sauce
a dash of Tabasco or
  chipotle Tabasco

METHOD

1. Preheat the oven to its lowest temperature.

2. Place the flour, paprika and baking powder in a large bowl. Add the milk and beaten eggs and whisk everything together well. Stir in the sweetcorn, spring onions, courgette, chilli and coriander and season with salt.

3. Heat a frying pan over a medium heat. Add a little oil or low-calorie oil spray to the pan and then add 2 dessertspoonfuls of the mixture per fritter. You will be able to get about three fritters in the pan at any one time. Fry for 3 minutes on each side, then place on a baking tray and keep warm in the low oven while you cook the rest of the batter, adding a little more oil as needed.

4. Mix together the crème fraîche, sweet chilli sauce and Tabasco in a small bowl, then serve the spicy crème fraîche with a stack of sweetcorn fritters and some rocket leaves.

Serves 4 / Prep 5 minutes / Cook 50 minutes /

Mexican Baked Sweet Potatoes

Baked potatoes always remind me of canteens, slightly dry potatoes topped with cheese that doesn't melt, or tuna and sweetcorn, or luke-warm baked beans, but this recipe is totally different, so give it a go and see how interesting they can be.

INGREDIENTS

4 sweet potatoes, washed
1 tbsp chipotle chilli paste
1 tbsp olive oil
1 red onion, sliced
2 peppers (ideally
  different colours), sliced
1 garlic clove, sliced
100g (3½oz) baby corn,
  each cut into 3 on the
  diagonal
½ tsp dried oregano
1 tsp chipotle paste
200g (7oz) spinach
salt
handful of snipped chives,
  to serve
chive sour cream, to
  serve (see page 124)

METHOD

1. Preheat the oven to 200°C (180°C fan/400°F/Gas 6).

2. Make cuts into each potato at 1cm (½in) intervals, as if slicing them into discs, but taking care not to go all the way through, so the potatoes stay in one piece.

3. Place the potatoes on a baking tray and bake in the oven for 40 minutes.

4. After 40 minutes spread the chipotle paste between the gaps in the potatoes and season with a little salt. Bake for a further 10 minutes.

5. While the potato finishes off in the oven, add the oil to a frying pan. Stir-fry the onion, peppers, garlic and corn together for 2 minutes, then sprinkle in the dried oregano and add the chipotle paste and spinach. Fry for another minute and season with salt.

6. Serve the potatoes with the stir-fried veggies and a spoonful of the chive sour cream, and finish with some chopped chives sprinkled over.

Serves 4 / Prep 15 minutes (plus cooling) / Cook 20 minutes / 584 kcal, 32g fat, 51g carbs, 19g protein

Mexican Bowl Chopped Salad

This is exactly what it says on the tin: a salad where everything is chopped into a uniform size and where anything goes. You can literally put anything in the salad, so get creative and use up any leftovers you might have in the kitchen.

INGREDIENTS

4 tortilla wraps
1 tsp olive oil
100g (3½oz) cooking
  chorizo, sliced
1 pepper (any colour)
5cm (2in) piece cucumber
2 large tomatoes
1 avocado, peeled, stone
  removed and diced
3 tbsp sweetcorn
400g can mixed beans,
  drained and rinsed
2 spring onions, sliced
small handfuls of parsley
  and coriander, chopped
4 tbsp sour cream
handful of grated cheese

DRESSING

2 tbsp olive oil
juice of 2 limes
2 tsp honey
1 tsp chopped fresh chilli

*1-litre (1¾-pint) Pyrex or
  other ovenproof bowl*

METHOD

1. Preheat the oven to 160°C (140°C fan/325°F/Gas 3).

2. Brush the tortilla wraps with a little oil on both sides. Press a tortilla wrap into the centre of the Pyrex bowl, so that it looks like a lining to the bowl.

3. Bake in the oven for 4–6 minutes until lightly golden brown, then remove and allow to cool. As it cools, it will crisp up. Remove it from the bowl and you will be left with a tortilla bowl. Repeat with the remaining wraps.

4. Place the sliced chorizo in a cold frying pan and turn on the heat. Fry until crispy, then drain off any excess fat and set aside.

5. Mix together the dressing ingredients in a small bowl.

6. Dice the pepper, cucumber and tomatoes and place in a large bowl with the avocado, sweetcorn, beans, spring onions and cooked chorizo. Mix together with the parsley and coriander and enough dressing to taste, but not to make it wet.

7. Divide the salad between the tortilla bowls and serve with a dollop of sour cream and a little grated cheese.

Serves 6 / Prep 5 minutes / Cook 35 minutes / 401 kcal, 13g fat, 26g carbs, 40g protein

Chilli Con Carne Bowl

This is a bit of a twist on a chilli con carne, as you can find that in lots of other books. So this is a nod to Mexican flavours but with a shorter cooking time.

INGREDIENTS

1 tbsp olive oil
1 onion, chopped
1 pepper, diced
1 garlic clove, chopped
2 tsp smoked paprika
1 tsp ground coriander
500g (1lb 2oz) minced
  beef
250g (9oz) mushrooms
400g can chopped
  tomatoes
1 tbsp chilli sauce
500ml (16fl oz) beef or
  chicken stock
400g can kidney beans (or
  mixed beans), drained
  and rinsed
200g (7oz) sweetcorn,
  canned or frozen

TO SERVE

100g (3½oz) cherry
  tomatoes, sliced
½ red onion, chopped, or
  2 spring onions, chopped
handful of grated cheese
lime wedges

METHOD

1. Heat the oil in a saucepan. Add the onion and pepper and cook for 5 minutes until starting to soften and turn lightly golden brown.

2. Stir in the garlic, paprika and coriander and cook for 30 seconds. Crumble in the beef and turn it over in the spices. Allow the beef to brown all over, then add in the mushrooms. Once the mushrooms start to soften, pour in the chopped tomatoes, chilli sauce, stock and beans. Bring everything to a simmer, then stir in the sweetcorn and simmer without a lid for 20 minutes, stirring occasionally.

3. After the 20 minutes, spoon into bowls and serve scattered with the chopped fresh cherry tomatoes, red onion or spring onions and grated cheese. Serve each portion with a wedge of lime on the side.

Serves 4 / Prep 25 minutes / Cook 15 minutes / 488 kcal, 12g fat, 17g carbs, 33g protein

Spicy Fish with Pineapple Salsa

This dish oozes sunshine. Spicy pan-fried fish with fruity salsa and not to forget the jazzed up rice that goes with it. Use white fish, such as cod, sea bass or haddock for this dish.

INGREDIENTS

2 tbsp olive oil
1 onion, chopped
200g (7oz) long-grain rice
400g can chopped
  tomatoes
1 tsp chilli powder
600ml (1 pint) chicken or
  vegetable stock
salt
2 tbsp sun-dried tomato
  paste
1 garlic clove, chopped
1 tsp dried oregano
1 tsp chopped fresh chilli
4 x 150g (5oz) white fish
  fillets, skin-on

SALSA

1 small pineapple, skin
  and core removed
1 small red onion
1 red chilli
2 spring onions
large handful of mint
juice of 2 limes
1 tbsp olive oil

METHOD

1. For the salsa, cut the pineapple into fine dice. Finely chop the onion, chilli, spring onions and mint, then mix with the pineapple, lime juice and olive oil. Season with a little salt and set aside.

2. Heat 1 tbsp of the oil in a saucepan which has a lid. Add the onion and fry for 1 minute. Add the rice, stirring it well to coat it in the oil. Add the tomatoes and chilli powder and bring to a simmer. Stir well, then pour in the stock and season with a pinch of salt. Cover the pan with a lid and simmer gently for 10 minutes or until all the stock has been absorbed. Remove it from the heat and leave it to stand for 5 minutes, then fluff up the rice with a fork.

3. Mix together the sun-dried tomato paste, garlic, oregano and chopped chilli. Brush the flesh side of the fish fillets with the mixture.

4. Heat the remaining 1 tbsp oil in a large frying pan over a medium-high heat. Fry the fish, skin-side down, for 3 minutes, depending on how thick the fillets are. Once you can see the fish starting to cook around the outside, turn the fish over and cook for 1 minute more.

5. Scatter with fish with the coriander and serve with the spicy rice and pineapple salsa.

THE DINER

KETCHUP

MUSTARD

The Diner

I love American diner food. It's delicious and, I think, a lot of fun. I have quite a romantic view of them, with the little tomato-shaped ketchup bottles, endless coffee, big burgers and stacks of pancakes... delicious. I remember going to a place when I was a child, which no longer exists, called Star Burger and my dad bought me a coke float. It was the first time I tried anything like it and I was amazed. This memory has always stayed with me and I think of it fondly, but the reality was we were probably enjoying very greasy food alongside it!

The recipes in this chapter are just as tasty as their restaurant counterparts, but come with much less, salt, fat and sugar. Find healthier versions of burger bar or American diner classics. Think chips, burgers, fries, pancakes and much more. My advice is to try to make it fun, get some paper chip cases or colourful napkins and make it an event at home.

Serves 4 / Prep 10 minutes / Cook 10 minutes / 438 kcal, 17g fat, 31g carbs, 39g protein

Beef Burgers

Once you remove the fat from meat, especially burgers, they become tasteless and dry. By adding a few breadcrumbs, moisture is held within the burger, and some garlic helps with the flavour. Spice everything up with my homemade burger sauce!

INGREDIENTS

1 slice bread, crusts removed
1 tbsp milk
500g (1lb 2 oz) finely minced beef
2 garlic cloves, crushed
2 tsp Dijon mustard
2 spring onions, very finely chopped
1 egg, beaten
salt and pepper
vegetable oil, for brushing
4 slices burger cheese
4 burger buns
handful of chopped iceberg lettuce
1 beef tomato, sliced
pickled gherkins, sliced

METHOD

1. To make the burger sauce, mix all the ingredients together and season with salt and pepper. Set aside.

2. Soak the bread in the milk until soft, then squeeze out any excess milk and place the bread in a bowl. Add the minced beef, garlic, mustard, spring onions and beaten egg and mix together. Season well with salt and pepper.

3. Divide the mince into four balls and flatten into patties (do not make them too compact). They will shrink when cooked, so make them about 15mm (½in) thick.

4. Preheat the grill to a high heat.

5. Brush both sides of the burgers with oil, then season with a little more salt and pepper. Place them on a rack with a baking tray underneath and grill for 3 minutes on each side or until golden brown. Once cooked, add a slice of cheese to each and grill for a further minute to melt it. Leave to rest for a couple of minutes.

6. Slice the burger buns in half and pop them under the grill, cut-side up, until golden.

7. Spread a little burger sauce (or any of your favourite sauces) on the bottom burger bun, add your patty, then stack it with crunchy lettuce, a slice of beef tomato and a few slices of gherkin. Serve and enjoy burger heaven.

BURGER SAUCE

1 tbsp tomato ketchup
2 tbsp mayonnaise
1 shallot, finely sliced
a few drops of Tabasco
1 tsp capers, drained and
   chopped (optional)
salt and pepper

Serves 4 / Prep 15 minutes / Cook 15 minutes / 406 kcal, 13g fat, 47g carbs, 23g protein

Veggie Burgers

My wife is a vegetarian and also a coeliac, and she loves these veggie burgers! Buy gluten-free burger buns and breadcrumbs to make them gluten-free.

INGREDIENTS

1 tbsp vegetable oil
1 small onion, finely chopped
175g (6oz) meat-free mince
40g (1½oz) grated cheese
75g (2½oz) plain yogurt
1 tbsp yeast extract dissolved in a splash of boiling water
2 tsp garlic granules
1 tsp onion salt
1 egg, beaten
breadcrumbs made from 2 slices bread or 100g (3½oz) shop-bought breadcrumbs
salt and pepper
4 cheese slices (optional)
4 burger buns
Little Gem lettuce leaves
1 beef tomato, sliced
mayonnaise
tomato ketchup
chilli sauce

METHOD

1. Heat a little of the oil in a frying pan, add the chopped onion and allow it to soften – you don't want it to colour. Allow to cool.

2. In a large mixing bowl, mix the cooked and cooled onion, meat-free mince, grated cheese, plain yogurt, yeast extract, garlic granules, onion salt, beaten egg, breadcrumbs and some salt and pepper.

3. Mix thoroughly and divide into four balls, then flatten into burger patties.

4. Heat the remaining oil in the pan you cooked the onions in and cook the burgers for 4–5 minutes on each side until they are golden and cooked through.

5. If you want, you can stick a slice of cheese on each burger for the last minute or two of cooking and allow it to melt.

6. Meanwhile, preheat the grill to a high heat. Slice the burger buns in half and pop them under the grill, cut-side up, until golden.

7. Serve each burger in a toasted bun with some Little Gem, tomato, mayo, ketchup and chilli sauce or whatever you fancy... I'm having a big dollop of chilli sauce and mayo with mine!

Serves 4 / Prep 15 minutes (plus marinating) / Cook 25 minutes / 573 kcal, 20g fat, 49g carbs, 46g protein

Crispy Chicken Burgers

Want it spicy? You got it! I love a chicken burger and this version is an indulgent classic. I cook mine in the oven rather than frying it, which makes it healthier for me, too. This is my favourite way to put together a chicken burger, but you can add cheese, bacon or tomato, if you like.

INGREDIENTS

4 chicken breasts
300ml (10fl oz) buttermilk,
  or use 300ml (10fl oz)
  milk and 1 tbsp lemon
  juice
100g (3½oz) plain flour
2 tsp cayenne pepper or
  paprika (you can leave it
  out if cooking for kids)
1 tsp garlic powder
salt and pepper
1–2 tbsp vegetable oil
4 burger buns, halved
4 tbsp mayonnaise mixed
  with 2 tbsp Sriracha hot
  sauce or sweet chilli
  sauce
¼ iceberg lettuce,
  shredded
2 gherkins, sliced
1 avocado, peeled, stone
  removed and sliced

*baking tray, lined with
  baking parchment*

METHOD

1. Put the chicken breasts between two sheets of clingfilm and give them a good bash with a rolling pin. We are trying to get the chicken to about 2cm (¾in) thick.

2. Put the buttermilk into a bowl and add the chicken. Leave it covered in the buttermilk for 1–2 hours.

3. Preheat the oven to 220°C (200°C fan/425°F/Gas 7).

4. In a large bowl or deep tray, mix together the flour, cayenne pepper, garlic powder and salt and pepper.

5. Take the chicken and shake off any excess buttermilk, then thoroughly coat the chicken in the seasoned flour.

6. Place the coated chicken breasts on the lined baking tray and drizzle with the oil. Put them in the oven and immediately reduce the oven temperature to 200°C (180°C fan/400°F/Gas 6).

7. Cook the chicken for 10 minutes, then reduce the temperature further to 180°C (160°C fan/350°F/Gas 4) and cook for a further 15 minutes. 1 minute before taking the chicken out of the oven, pop the halved burger buns, cut-side up on a baking tray and toast.

8. Spread a little of the spicy mayo on each bun, top with shredded lettuce, then the crispy chicken, gherkins, avocado and a little more of the spicy mayo. Top with the bun lid and serve.

Serves 4 / Prep 15 minutes / Cook 17 minutes / 454 kcal, 8.2g fat, 57g carbs, 37g protein

Popcorn Chicken with Pickled Shallots

These bite-sized pieces of chicken are sure to be a family favourite and they are a great recipe to get the kids to help with. Get them shaking the bags and coating the chicken while you enjoy a nice cuppa.

INGREDIENTS

3 large chicken breasts
120g (4oz) plain flour
1 tsp salt
1 tbsp fajita seasoning
  (optional)
2 large eggs, beaten
60ml (2fl oz) milk
100g (3½oz) cornflakes
sour cream, to serve

SHALLOTS

2 tbsp sugar
2 tbsp vinegar (ideally red
  wine vinegar, but any
  will do)
½ tsp crushed dried
  chillies
2 shallots, thinly sliced

*baking tray, lined with
  baking parchment*

METHOD

1. Preheat the oven to 200°C (180°C fan/400°F/Gas 6).

2. Cut the chicken into bite-sized pieces, about 1–1.5cm (½in), and place them in a zip-lock bag. Add the flour, salt and fajita seasoning, if using. Give everything a really good shake to coat the chicken.

3. In a bowl, whisk together the eggs and milk.

4. Place the cornflakes in another zip-lock bag and squeeze out all the air. Use a rolling pin to crush the cornflakes into small pieces.

5. Remove the chicken from the flour and shake off the excess. Place the chicken pieces in the egg and milk mixture, then shake off the excess and pop them into the bag with the crushed cornflakes. Shake to coat, then spread them out on the lined baking tray. Bake in the oven for 10 minutes, then turn them over and cook for a further 7 minutes.

6. While the chicken is cooking, heat together the sugar, vinegar and crushed dried chillies. When the sugar has dissolved, add the shallot rings and stir. Remove from the heat and allow to cool.

7. When the chicken is cooked, remove from the oven. Drain the shallot rings. Serve the chicken scattered with shallot rings and drizzled with sour cream.

Serves 4 / Prep 15 minutes / Cook 20 minutes / 584 kcal, 20g fat, 56g carbs, 43g protein

Fillet of Fish

We love fast food because it is tasty, hot and fast. I have always said that, for me, fish is the ultimate fast food, as it cooks so quickly.

INGREDIENTS

80g (3oz) plain flour
½ tsp cayenne pepper
  or paprika
salt and pepper
4 cod fillets (can be
  frozen and defrosted,
  but defrost them
  on a few pieces of
  kitchen paper to absorb
  all the water)
2 eggs, beaten
120g (4oz) dried
  breadcrumbs
2 tbsp rapeseed oil
4 slices burger cheese
4 brioche burger buns,
  halved
Tartar Sauce (see page
  189), to serve
handful of rocket leaves,
  to serve

*baking tray, lined with
  baking parchment*

METHOD

1. Preheat the oven to 190°C (170°C fan/375°F/Gas 5).

2. Season the flour with the cayenne pepper or paprika and salt and pepper.

3. Dip the cod fillets in the flour, then the beaten egg, then the breadcrumbs to coat. If you want, you can repeat this process once more.

4. Lay the cod fillets on the lined baking tray, drizzle the oil over them and bake them in the oven for 15 minutes.

5. After 15 minutes, take them out of the oven, pop a slice of cheese onto each fillet of fish and cook for a further 1–2 minutes until the cheese is melted.

6. Toast the halved brioche buns under the grill, cut-side up, or in a dry frying pan, cut-side down.

7. Spread the base of the brioche buns with tartar sauce, then top with the fish fillets and the rocket leaves. Add the bun tops and serve.

Serves 6 / Prep 20 minutes (plus cooling) / Cook 35 minutes / 284 kcal, 7.4g fat, 42g carbs, 10g protein

Oat Pancakes

Pancakes are a classic American diner staple. I like to put oats in the batter as it helps fill you up for longer, making it a nutritious and delicious breakfast! The addition of banana in the mixture means you are getting an extra portion of fruit, before you have even topped them!

INGREDIENTS

2 eggs
175ml (6fl oz) milk
100g (3½oz) plain yogurt
225g (8oz) self-raising
  flour
50g (1¾oz) porridge oats
1 tsp baking powder
2 ripe bananas, peeled
  and mashed, handful of
  raisins, grated apple or
  blueberries (optional)
2 tbsp rapeseed oil or
  low-calorie oil spray

BERRY COMPOTE

300g (10oz) frozen berries
1 tsp vanilla paste or
  extract
1–2 tbsp honey, to taste

TO SERVE

4 heaped tbsp plain
  yogurt

METHOD

1. In a large bowl, whisk together the eggs, milk and yogurt, then add the flour, oats and baking powder. (Add the mashed banana, raisins, apple or blueberries now, if using.)

2. Heat a frying pan on a medium heat, add a little oil or low-calorie oil spray and dollop a generous tablespoon of the oat mixture into the middle. Cook for 2 minutes (if you are feeling adventurous and have a big enough pan, you can do a few at a time). Flip the pancake(s) over and cook for another 1–2 minutes.

3. Set aside and repeat with the rest of the mixture (you can always keep them warm in a low oven).

4. For the berry compote, place the berries (reserving a handful or so for later) in a saucepan along with the vanilla and honey. Turn the heat on and allow the berries to warm through. They will start to release their juices.

5. Once they have released their juices, bring them to a simmer and simmer gently for 20 minutes until thickened slightly. Take the pan off the heat, stir through the reserved berries and then leave to cool. Keep it in an airtight container in the fridge, ready to serve with your oat pancakes and a dollop of plain yogurt.

Serves 4–6 / 229 kcal, 7.7g fat, 35g carbs, 3.6g protein

Healthy Hash Browns

INGREDIENTS

4 large potatoes (Maris Piper or King
  Edward ideally), peeled and grated
1 onion, finely sliced or grated (optional)
salt and pepper
3 tbsp melted butter or vegetable oil

12-hole muffin tin, lightly greased

METHOD

1. Preheat the oven to 180°C (160°C
   fan/350°F/Gas 4).

2. Put the grated potatoes and onion in a
   bowl of cold salted water and give them
   a good mix around until the water turns
   cloudy. This will draw out a lot of the
   starch in the potatoes and soften the
   onions. Drain the potatoes in a sieve,
   then, using a clean tea towel, squeeze
   out as much water as you can.

3. Place the mixture back in the bowl
   and add the melted butter or oil, and
   season well with salt and pepper.

4. Divide the mixture evenly between
   the holes of the muffin tin. Bake in the
   oven for 40–45 minutes or until the
   potatoes are cooked and crispy. Serve
   with cooked eggs or cheese on top.

Serves 4 / 235 kcal, 6.6g fat, 29g carbs, 14g protein

Egg Muffins

INGREDIENTS

4 eggs
salt and pepper
4 English muffins, halved
toppings of your choice, such as chopped
  chillies, sliced spring onions, grated
  cheese, tomatoes, mushrooms, avocado
  or spinach leaves

6-hole muffin tin, lightly greased

METHOD

1. Preheat the oven to 180°C (160°C
   fan/350°F/Gas 4).

2. Crack an egg into four holes of the
   greased muffin tin, season with salt
   and pepper and bake in the oven for
   5–6 minutes until the egg white is firm.
   Meanwhile, toast the muffins.

3. When the eggs are cooked, use a
   spatula to loosen them and then pop
   them out of the muffin tin.

4. Place an egg on the base of each
   toasted muffin, then top with your
   favourite toppings. Cheese, chillies
   and a few baby spinach leaves for me!
   Pop the muffin lids back on and pop
   them back in the oven on a baking tray
   for 2 minutes to warm through. Serve.

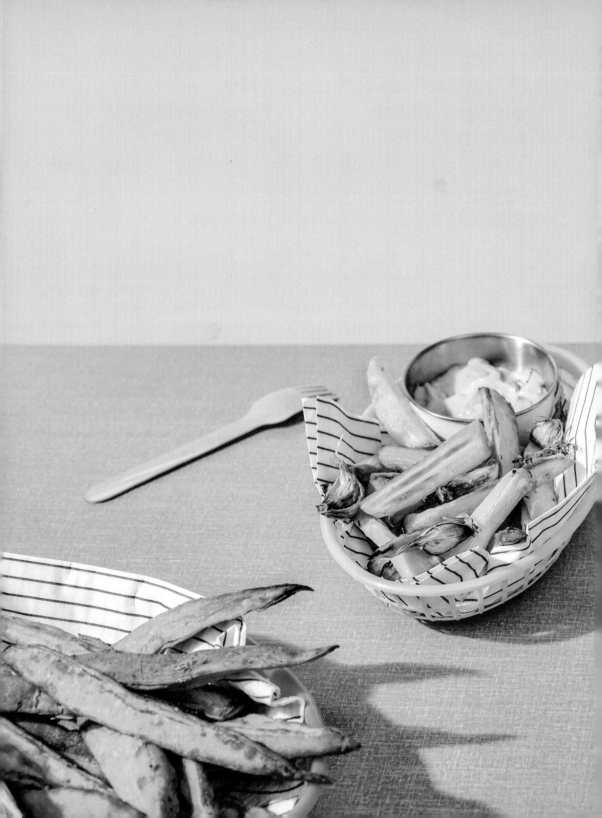

Chips, Chips, Chips DF GF VE V

Who doesn't like chips? They don't have to be unhealthy or just plain old potatoes. However, when you remove some of the fat by baking them rather than frying them, they do need a bit of a flavour boost. Here are my three favourite recipes that go with almost anything.

Serves 4 / 198 kcal, 3.4g fat, 37g carbs, 2.2g protein

Sweet Potato & Paprika Wedges

INGREDIENTS

4 large sweet potatoes, scrubbed and
  cut into wedges
1 tbsp vegetable oil
1 tsp smoked paprika
salt

baking tray, lined with baking parchment

METHOD

1. Preheat the oven to 180°C (160°C fan/350°F/Gas 4).

2. Place the wedges in a bowl and add the oil, paprika and a pinch of salt. Toss everything together, then spread the wedges out evenly over the lined baking tray.

3. Bake in the oven for 40 minutes, turning halfway through. Serve.

Serves 4 / 211 kcal, 5.7g fat, 35g carbs, 3.6g protein

Skinny Chips with Rosemary Salt

INGREDIENTS

4 large floury potatoes, peeled and cut into skinny chips
2 tbsp olive oil
1 tsp sea salt
1 tsp finely chopped rosemary

baking tray, lined with baking parchment

METHOD

1. Preheat the oven to 180°C (160°C fan/350°F/Gas 4).

2. Place the chips in a bowl of cold water and swish them about. This will help remove some of the starch. Drain them and then place them on a clean tea towel and pat dry.

3. Place the dried chips onto the lined baking tray and drizzle over the oil. Mix them around a bit so that the chips are covered in the oil, then spread them out.

4. Bake in the oven for 25 minutes, turning halfway through.

5. Mix together the salt and rosemary, then sprinkle it over the chips and bake for a further 5 minutes.

Serves 4–6 / 189 kcal, 6.4g fat, 26g carbs, 3.6g protein

Veggie Chips with Thyme & Garlic

INGREDIENTS

2 large parsnips, peeled and cut into 5mm (¼in) thick chips
2 carrots, peeled and cut into 5mm (¼in) thick chips
2 potatoes, peeled and cut into 5mm (¼in) thick chips
2 tbsp olive oil
salt
a few sprigs of thyme, leaves picked
bulb of garlic, cloves separated and lightly crushed

baking tray, lined with baking parchment

METHOD

1. Preheat the oven to 180°C (160°C fan/350°F/Gas 4).

2. Place all the veg in a large bowl with the oil, sprinkle with salt and the thyme leaves, and add the garlic cloves. Mix together, then spread them out evenly over the lined baking tray.

3. Bake in the oven for 40 minutes, turning halfway through.

Serves 2 / 122 kcal, 0.5g fat, 23g carbs, 3.0g protein

Make-Your-Own Milkshakes

We all loved milkshakes as kids, but mainly because they were often made with ice cream and packed full of sugar! However, these days they can be healthy and there are lots of ways to make them your own. Simply change the milk or fruit to one of your liking, or try adding a shot of coffee into a chocolate shake for a real boost! Here are three of my top flavours, or you can follow the recipes on the right.

INGREDIENTS

300ml (10fl oz) milk of
  your choice
2 tbsp plain yogurt
2 tsp vanilla extract or
  vanilla bean paste
2 bananas, peeled

FLAVOURING OPTIONS

2 tbsp peanut butter
2 handfuls of blueberries
2 handfuls of frozen
  cherries
1 tbsp chocolate spread
  or 1 tbsp chocolate
  powder
2 handfuls of frozen or
  fresh strawberries/
  raspberries
1 tbsp honey
a dash of milk, to loosen,
  if needed

METHOD

1. Blitz together the base ingredients in a blender until smooth. Then you can add any of the flavourings into the blend and simply blitz it up!

Serves 2 / 176 kcal, 3g fat, 30g carbs, 7g protein

Banana & Vanilla Milkshake

INGREDIENTS

2 bananas, peeled
1 tsp vanilla extract or vanilla bean paste
1 tsp honey
300ml (10fl oz) milk of your choice
½ tsp ground cinnamon
a few ice cubes

METHOD

1. Place everything in a blender and blitz.

Serves 2 / 189 kcal, 3.8g fat, 28g carbs, 9.6g protein

Berry Milkshake

INGREDIENTS

350ml (12fl oz) skimmed milk
1 large ripe banana
150g (5½oz) fresh or frozen mixed berries
100g (3½oz) yogurt (plain or strawberry)
a squeeze of honey (optional)

METHOD

1. Place everything in a blender and blitz.

Serves 2 / 207 kcal, 11g fat, 17g carbs, 10g protein

Choconut Milkshake

INGREDIENTS

1 banana, peeled
2 tbsp cocoa powder
2 tbsp peanut butter
200ml (7fl oz) milk of your choice (I like
    using unsweetened almond or
    unsweetened coconut milk for this one,
    but any milk works)
a few ice cubes

METHOD

1. Place everything in a blender and blitz.

Serves 4 / Prep 25 minutes / Cook 25 minutes / 330 kcal, 7.0g fat, 58g carbs, 5.6g protein

Apple Pies

The apple pie from the well-known burger place is actually fried, but that is a no-no for me. This is my lighter version, packed full of fruity goodness with a bit of cinnamon spice.

INGREDIENTS

2 cooking apples, peeled, cored and thinly sliced
2 eating apples, peeled, cored and thinly sliced
juice of ½ lemon
75g (2½oz) caster sugar
1 tsp ground cinnamon
1 tsp vanilla bean paste or extract
1 tsp cornflour
4 sheets filo pastry
25g (1oz) butter, melted
icing sugar, for sprinkling
plain yogurt, to serve

baking sheet, lined with baking parchment

METHOD

1. Preheat the oven to 190°C (170°C fan/375°F/Gas 5).

2. Place the sliced apples in a bowl and add the lemon juice, caster sugar, cinnamon, vanilla and cornflour and mix everything together.

3. Take a sheet of filo pastry and brush one side with melted butter. Spoon one-quarter of the apple mixture in a line along the short side of the sheet, leaving a little bit of pastry free at each end. Fold the ends in and then roll the pastry up to enclose the apple mixture. Brush the outside with butter and pop it on the lined baking sheet. Repeat with the remaining apple mixture and filo sheets.

4. Bake them in the oven for 15–20 minutes, then remove from the oven and sprinkle with icing sugar. Serve with plain yogurt.

Chicken Shop

In recent years we have seen chicken restaurants move from fast food outlets to the casual dining scene. They are hugely popular and serve food that's full of flavour. Whether your chicken of choice comes with secret herbs and spices or a pretty famous sauce that is so good they named it twice, you will find some delicious versions of your favourite chicken dishes here. What could be better than some lovely chicken, with healthy sides of coleslaw, rice, corn on the cob and lots of other vegetarian options? These dishes pack a punch, but don't worry, you can choose to make it as spicy as you like. Lots of the recipes in this chapter are really quick and can be made gluten-free.

Serves 4–6 / Prep 15 minutes (plus marinating) / Cook 40 minutes / 326 kcal, 17g fat, 6.8g carbs, 34g protein

Chicken Wings

These are hot, hot, hot! I would recommend going to your butcher and getting them to do some of the work by halving the wings and removing the wing tips, if you are not confident to do so. These wings are nice served with spicy rice, salad or corn on the cob... or all of them!

INGREDIENTS

4 garlic cloves, crushed
3 small red Birdseye
    chillies (or other chillies,
    but be mindful as they
    vary in strength)
2 tsp salt
2 tsp black pepper
grated zest and juice of
    1 lemon
2 tbsp olive oil
1 red onion, finely
    chopped
2 tsp paprika
1 red pepper, finely
    chopped
1 tbsp white wine vinegar
1kg (2lb) whole chicken
    wings, cut in half
    through the joint and the
    wing tips removed
finely sliced spring
    onions, to serve

*large baking tray, lined
    with baking parchment*

METHOD

1. Blitz the garlic, chillies, salt, pepper, lemon zest and juice, olive oil, red onion, paprika, red pepper and vinegar together in a food processor or with a stick blender. (If you don't have either of these bits of kit, don't worry. You can soften the onion and pepper in a pan with a little oil, then add the other ingredients. Cook on a medium heat for a couple of minutes, you can then choose to sieve out the onion or leave it in for a bit of texture!)

2. Once you have your sauce made to the consistency you like, remove a few spoonfuls and set aside for later. To the rest of the sauce, add the wings and turn to coat, then leave to marinate for at least 20 minutes, but as long as you can, ideally overnight.

3. Preheat the oven to 180°C (160°C fan/350°F/Gas 4).

4. Spread the wings out on the lined baking tray and bake in the oven for 40 minutes until cooked through.

5. After 30 minutes, take them out and brush them with the reserved sauce you set aside. Cook for the final 10 minutes, then serve with a sprinkling of spring onions on top.

Serves 4 / Prep 5 minutes (plus marinating) / Cook 10 minutes / 472 kcal, 19g fat, 38g carbs, 36g protein

Chilli Chicken Wraps

INGREDIENTS

3 chicken breasts, each
  cut into 4 long strips
2 tbsp sweet chilli sauce
pinch of crushed dried
  chillies, or a little
  chopped fresh chilli
grated zest and juice of
  1 lime
1 avocado
½ small red onion, finely
  chopped, or 2 spring
  onions, chopped
salt and pepper
4 tortilla wraps, warmed
4 tbsp crème fraîche or
  plain yogurt
handful of rocket leaves
  or other salad leaves

METHOD

1. Place the strips of chicken breast into a bowl. Add the sweet chilli sauce, chilli, all the lime zest and half the lime juice and mix together, coating the chicken. Leave to marinate for 30 minutes if you can.

2. When ready to serve, cook the marinated chicken strips in a large grill pan over a medium heat. Cook for 5 minutes until brown, then turn over to cook through.

3. Meanwhile, cut the avocado in half. Remove the stone, then use a spoon to scoop out the flesh. Cut the avocado flesh into small cubes. Place them in a bowl, then squeeze over the remaining lime juice and stir in the onion or spring onions. Season with salt and pepper.

4. For each serving, place a warm tortilla wrap on a board. Add a dollop of crème fraîche and spread it out. Scatter over a few rocket or salad leaves, then place three strips of chicken down the centre of the wrap. Spoon over some of the avocado mix, then tuck in the ends, roll up and enjoy.

Serves 4 / Prep 15 minutes / Cook 50 minutes / 327 kcal, 10g fat, 24g carbs, 31g protein

Tasty Chicken Tray Bake

I much prefer chicken thighs over chicken breasts. They take longer to cook, but the meat has much more flavour and is less prone to drying out. Roasting them with a few vegetables means it's a meal in one.

INGREDIENTS

6–8 boneless chicken thigh fillets (skin-on)
2 tbsp olive oil
3 tsp crushed dried chillies, or 2 chillies, chopped
4 garlic cloves
grated zest and juice of 1 lime
2 tsp dried oregano
1 tsp cayenne pepper
½ tsp salt
½ tsp black pepper
200g (7oz) cherry tomatoes (on the vine if possible)
1 aubergine, cut into 1cm (½in) cubes
1 courgette, cut into 1cm (½in) cubes
1 red onion, cut into wedges
2 sweet potatoes, peeled and cut into 1cm (½in) cubes

METHOD

1. Preheat the oven to 180°C (160°C fan/350°F/Gas 4).

2. Score the skins of the chicken thighs and set aside. Mix all the remaining ingredients together in a bowl, add the chicken and toss to make sure the chicken is covered in the mixture.

3. Transfer everything to a baking tray and spoon out any leftover mixture from the bowl onto the chicken. Bake the chicken mixture in the oven for 50 minutes, or until cooked thoroughly. Serve. The chicken in this recipe works beautifully on the barbecue, too.

Serves 6 / Prep 25 minutes (plus marinating) / Cook 40 minutes (plus resting) / 340 kcal, 18g fat, 11g carbs, 34g protein

Jerk Chicken

I'm going to do this recipe as a spatchcock chicken, as I think it's the best of both worlds – you enjoy a whole chicken, but it cooks in less time. However, you can just flavour a whole chicken, if you prefer; just amend the cooking times. You can also use various other cuts of chicken.

INGREDIENTS

6 spring onions, chopped
1 tbsp vegetable oil
4cm (1¾in) piece fresh
  root ginger, grated
4 garlic cloves, chopped
  or crushed
1 onion, chopped
2 Scotch Bonnet chilles
½ tsp thyme (chopped
  fresh or dried)
grated zest and juice of
  1 lime
2 tbsp soy sauce
2 tbsp light brown sugar
1 tbsp ground allspice
½ tbsp salt
1.5kg (3lb 3oz) whole
  chicken

METHOD

1. Blend the spring onions, oil, ginger, garlic, onion, chillies, thyme, lime zest and juice, soy sauce, brown sugar, allspice and salt in a food processor or use a stick blender. You can just mix them all together in a bowl – you won't get it to a smooth paste, but that's ok.

2. To spatchcock the chicken, place the chicken breast-side down with the legs towards you. Using kitchen scissors, cut up along each side of the backbone, starting at the parson's nose (the little fleshy stub at the end of the chicken). Do this on both sides and remove the backbone, then turn the chicken over and flatten it with the palm of your hand (think CPR, although there is no hope at this stage!).

3. Reserve some of the sauce for basting and spread the rest of the sauce all over the chicken and under the skin. Leave in the fridge (covered) for up to 24 hours.

4. When you are ready to cook, remove the chicken from the fridge and preheat the oven to 180°C (160°C fan/ 350°F/Gas 4).

5. Put the chicken on a baking tray, skin-side up, and cook for 20 minutes. After 20 minutes, take it out and brush it with the reserved sauce. Cook for a further 20 minutes until cooked through. Remove from the oven and leave to rest for at least 10 minutes before serving.

Makes 4 / Prep 15 minutes / Cook 10 minutes / 439 kcal, 9.3g fat, 63g carbs, 18g protein

Bean Burgers

V

These burgers are a great storecupboard recipe, so they can be made on any night of the week. Beans are a great source of fibre and can help slow the absorption of sugar into the blood, reducing blood sugar levels. All in all, it's a win-win.

INGREDIENTS

2 x 400g cans kidney beans
1 carrot, peeled and
  grated
1 onion, finely chopped
breadcrumbs made from
  2 slices bread
1 tsp onion salt
1 tsp garlic granules
1 tsp chilli powder
  (optional)
salt and pepper
small bunch of fresh
  coriander, finely
  chopped
1 egg, beaten
4 cheese slices (optional)
4 burger buns, halved and
  toasted
4 tbsp mayonnaise
2 tbsp sweet chilli sauce
Little Gem lettuce

*baking tray, greased with
vegetable oil or low-
calorie oil spray*

METHOD

1. Preheat the oven to 180°C (160°C fan/350°F/Gas 4).

2. Drain and rinse the kidney beans, then place them in a bowl and mash them with a potato masher (alternatively, you can blitz these in a food processor).

3. Add the carrot, onion, breadcrumbs, onion salt, garlic granules, chilli powder, salt and pepper, and the chopped coriander. Mix well and stir in the beaten egg.

4. Divide the mixture into four balls and then flatten out into burger patties. Place them on the greased baking tray and cook in the preheated oven for 10 minutes, turning them over halfway through.

5. If you want, you can pop a slice of cheese on each burger after 8 minutes and carry on cooking for the remaining 2 minutes, allowing it to melt.

6. Serve each burger in a toasted bun with the mayonnaise and sweet chilli sauce, and some crunchy lettuce leaves.

Serves 4 / 449 kcal, 30g fat, 17g carbs, 29g protein

Halloumi Fries

INGREDIENTS

2 x 225g packs of halloumi
75g (2½oz) plain flour or gluten-free plain
 flour
2 tsp smoked paprika
salt and pepper
vegetable oil, for shallow-frying

METHOD

1. Pull each block of halloumi apart into
   two pieces (it has a natural break in the
   middle), then slice into chips.

2. In a bowl, mix the together the flour,
   paprika and a pinch of salt and pepper,
   then use to coat the halloumi, shaking
   off any excess.

3. Add the oil to a the biggest frying pan
   you have. Try not to overcrowd the pan
   with halloumi chips (so you might have
   to do this in batches) and heat until
   sizzling. Fry for 1–2 minutes, turning
   with tongs, until golden and crispy all
   over. Transfer to a piece of kitchen
   paper and repeat with the remaining
   halloumi chips.

4. Sprinkle the fries with salt and serve
   with your favourite sauce to dip into.

Serves 12 / 284 kcal, 31g fat, 0.6g carbs, 0.4g protein

Butters for Corn-cobs

CHILLI & CORIANDER BUTTER

150g (5½oz) butter, softened
grated zest of 2 limes
1 chilli, finely chopped
2 tsp sea salt
handful of fresh coriander, finely chopped

LEMON & BLACK PEPPER BUTTER

150g (5½oz) butter, softened
grated zest of 2 lemons
1 tsp coarsely ground black pepper

TOMATO & GARLIC BUTTER

150g (5½oz) butter, softened
20g (¾oz) sun-dried tomatoes in oil,
 drained, finely chopped
1 garlic clove, finely chopped

METHOD

1. For each butter, mash the butter until
   soft, then mix with the other
   ingredients. Chill the butter in the
   fridge in the bowl you mixed it in or, if
   you want it in a nice roll, place the
   butter in a line down the edge of a
   double-sheet of clingfilm, then roll it
   up into a sausage. These butters will
   keep in the fridge for 5 days. Melt them
   all over cooked corn for flavour!.

Serves 4 / 438 kcal, 12g fat, 72g carbs, 7.7g protein

Chilli Salt Fries

INGREDIENTS

4 large floury potatoes (such as Maris
  Piper), cut into thin chips
2 tbsp vegetable oil

CHILLI SALT

3 tbsp sea salt
1½ tbsp paprika
2 tbsp dried thyme
1 tbsp garlic granules
½ tbsp sugar
1 tbsp crushed dried chillies

METHOD

1. Put the chilli salt ingredients into a
   pestle and mortar, and crush into a
   fine powder. Store in an airtight jar.

2. Preheat the oven to 190°C (170°C
   fan/375°F/Gas 5).

3. Place the potatoes in a bowl of cold
   water and mix around. Drain and pat
   dry on a clean tea towel. Place the
   dried potatoes in a bowl and mix with
   the vegetable oil and 2 tbsp of the chilli
   salt. Mix well. Tip the potatoes onto a
   baking tray and spread them out.

4. Cook in the oven for 40–45 minutes
   until crispy, shaking halfway through.

Serves 4 / 92 kcal, 5.9g fat, 6.5g carbs, 1.6g protein

Piri Piri Sauce

INGREDIENTS

4 garlic cloves
3 red chillies (you can use any chillies,
  but be mindful as they vary in strength,
  so you might need to adjust the amount
  depending on the heat)
1 red pepper, chopped
1½ tsp salt
2 tsp freshly ground black pepper
grated zest and juice of 1 lemon
2 tbsp olive oil
1 red onion, chopped
2 tsp hot smoked paprika
1 tbsp white wine vinegar
½ tsp dried oregano (optional)

METHOD

1. Put all the ingredients into a food
   processor or blender and whizz
   together. You can use a stick blender
   for this as well.

2. If you are using this as a marinade, just
   use it as is. If you are using this as a dip
   or table sauce, then you want to heat
   the sauce in a pan on a low heat with a
   lid on for 10–12 minutes – add a splash
   of water, if it's too thick.

Serves 4 / Prep 5 minutes / Cook 20 minutes / 360 kcal, 4.3g fat, 69g carbs, 8.3g protein

Spicy Rice

This is delicious and super easy. You can make a bigger batch and keep it in the fridge, or freeze it once cooled for another day. Feel free to add any other veggies to this that you like, such as celery, mushrooms, sweetcorn... whatever you have in the fridge that needs using up.

INGREDIENTS

1 tbsp rapeseed or
  vegetable oil
1 onion, finely chopped
1 garlic clove, crushed or
  finely chopped
1 red pepper, finely
  chopped
1 tsp paprika
1 tsp ground turmeric
½ tsp crushed dried
  chillies or chilli powder
300g (10oz) long-grain
  rice
600ml (1 pint) vegetable
  stock
salt and pepper
100g (3½oz) frozen peas
handful of green beans,
  chopped

METHOD

1. You will be doing this all in one pan, so it's best to use the biggest saucepan you have.

2. Heat the oil in the pan and add the onion. Fry for 4–5 minutes until soft, but not coloured.

3. Add the garlic, red pepper, paprika, turmeric and crushed dried chillies or chilli powder and mix well. Cook the spices out for a couple of minutes.

4. Add the rice and the stock, then season well with salt and pepper.

5. Bring to the boil, cover with a lid and turn the heat down. Cook for 8–9 minutes, or until the rice is almost cooked.

6. Add the peas and green beans and stir through. Cover and leave on a low heat for another 1 minute, then turn off the heat and leave to stand for 3 minutes with the lid still on. You want the rice to be cooked but the beans still crunchy.

Serves 6 / 88 kcal, 2.9g fat, 11g carbs, 2.5g protein

Classic Coleslaw with a Twist

INGREDIENTS

2 tbsp yogurt
2 tbsp mayonnaise
1 tbsp horseradish sauce
2 carrots, peeled and finely grated
½ red onion, thinly sliced
½ white cabbage, thinly sliced
1 tbsp chopped fresh dill or chives
salt and pepper

METHOD

1. Mix together all the ingredients in a bowl, seasoning well with salt and pepper, then serve.

Serves 6 / 174 kcal, 13g fat, 9.2g carbs, 3.0g protein

Winter Cabbage Slaw

INGREDIENTS

2 tbsp olive oil
juice of ½ lemon
1 tsp honey
salt and pepper
½ red cabbage, thinly sliced
¼ cauliflower, finely chopped
1 eating apple, cored and grated
2 celery sticks, finely chopped
40g (1½oz) pecans
a few Parmesan shavings (optional)

METHOD

1. In a large bowl, mix together the oil, lemon juice and honey with a little salt and pepper.

2. Stir in the cabbage, cauliflower, apple and celery. Coat everything in the dressing.

3. hen ready to serve, sprinkle with pecans and Parmesan shavings, if using.

Green Slaw with Mint

Waldorf Slaw

INGREDIENTS

2 tbsp mayonnaise
2 tbsp crème fraîche or plain yogurt
grated zest and juice of 1 lime
a pinch of sugar, or a drizzle of honey
salt and pepper
1 small bulb of fennel, thinly sliced
½ small white cabbage, thinly sliced"
100g (3½oz) frozen peas, defrosted
2 celery sticks, sliced
1 green eating apple, cored and thinly
  sliced
1 tbsp chopped fresh mint
1 tbsp chopped fresh chives

METHOD

1. In a large bowl, mix together the
   mayonnaise, crème fraîche or yogurt,
   lime zest and juice with a pinch of
   sugar, or a drizzle of honey, and season
   with salt and pepper.

2. Stir in the veggies, apple and herbs,
   then serve.

INGREDIENTS

2 tbsp fat-free Greek yogurt
1 tsp apple cider vinegar
drizzle of olive oil
1 tsp honey
salt and pepper
1 red onion, thinly sliced
¼ large red cabbage, thinly sliced
2 celery sticks, thinly sliced
2 eating apples, preferably Granny Smith,
  cored and sliced into matchsticks
100g (3½oz) raisins (soaked in 3 tbsp
  apple juice if you can)
100g (3½oz) chopped walnuts

METHOD

1. In a large bowl, mix the yogurt, vinegar,
   oil and honey together, then season
   with salt and pepper.

2. Stir in all the veg and fruit, and top with
   the chopped walnuts, then serve .

The Chippy

The smell of chips covered in salt and vinegar is truly wonderful. This is a takeaway we did have when I was as a kid, not every week, but probably once a month or so. I used to be sent down to the chippy with the list of what everyone was having... waiting in the queue on a Friday night with that unforgettable smell.

I still love the idea of having fish and chips from a chip shop, but the reality is, it's too greasy for me now. There is no need to fry your fish and chips. By the time you cover it in your chosen condiments, you won't miss that extra oil at all! But you will save lots of calories and saturated fat.

If your local chip shop is a busy one, you might even be able to make your own healthy fish and chips in the time it takes to go down there, queue up and get it home! Fresher, healthier, faster and cheaper, Friday nights just got a lot better. All the recipes in this chapter can easily be adapted to be gluten-free.

Serves 4 / Prep 15 minutes / Cook 40 minutes / 396 kcal, 6.2g fat, 40g carbs, 43g protein

Fish & New Potato 'Chips'

DF

This take on fish and chips uses cornflakes to coat the fish instead of batter. Ideally use fillets from the head end of the fish rather than the tail.

INGREDIENTS

100g (3½oz) cornflakes
½ tsp smoked paprika
  (optional)
2 tbsp finely chopped
  fresh parsley
2 eggs, lightly beaten
4 white fish fillets, such
  as haddock, about 200g
  (7oz) each

NEW POTATO CHIPS

500g (1lb 2oz) new
  potatoes, scrubbed
1 tbsp olive oil
salt and pepper
4 garlic cloves, lightly
  bruised with the blade
  of a knife
a few thyme leaves
grated zest of 1 lemon

*baking tray, lined with
  baking parchment*

METHOD

1. Preheat the oven to 200°C (180°C fan/400°F/Gas 6).

2. Start with the chips. Place a new potato in the 'cup' of a wooden spoon. With a sharp knife, make downward cuts into the potato at regular intervals; the more you do the crispier your potatoes will be. The spoon will stop you from cutting all the way through. You want the cuts in the potato to fan out while still held together.

3. Place the potatoes on a baking tray, drizzle with the oil and season with salt and pepper. Gently rub the oil and seasoning into each potato, then bake for 30 minutes.

4. Meanwhile, place the cornflakes in a bowl. Use a rolling pin to crush them into a fine crumb (you want some finely crushed, but it's ok to have some chunkier bits, too). Add the paprika, if using, and parsley.

5. Season the eggs with salt and pepper. Dip the fish fillets in the egg, then place in the crumb, pressing it firmly onto the fish. Place the fish on the lined baking tray and bake in the oven with the 'chips' for 15 minutes.

6. After the 'chips' have been cooking for 30 minutes, scatter the potatoes with the garlic and thyme leaves, and bake for a further 10 minutes.

7. Remove the potatoes from the oven and sprinkle with the lemon zest. Serve the 'chips' alongside the fish with a good wedge of lemon and a few salad leaves.

Healthy Baked 'Scampi'

Scampi is traditionally made with langoustines, but today they are super expensive, so good old raw king prawns will take their place. The little bit of coconut adds a bit of natural sweetness and interest to the scampi, but if you are not a fan, you can always leave it out.

INGREDIENTS

40g (1½oz) plain flour
1 tsp paprika
grated zest and juice of
 1 lemon
salt and pepper
2 eggs, beaten
120g (4oz) dried
 breadcrumbs or panko
 breadcrumbs
20g (¾oz) desiccated
 coconut
400g (14oz) peeled raw
 king prawns
1 tbsp olive oil
lemon wedges, to serve

*baking tray, lined with
 baking parchment*

METHOD

1. Preheat the oven to 200°C (180°C fan/400°F/Gas 6).

2. Put the flour, paprika and lemon zest in one bowl and season with salt and pepper.

3. Put the beaten eggs in another bowl and mix the breadcrumbs and coconut in a third bowl.

4. Individually dip the prawns first into the flour, then into the egg and then in the breadcrumbs to coat. Then place on the lined baking tray.

5. When you have coated all the prawns, drizzle over the oil and bake in the oven for 10 minutes until cooked and crispy.

6. Serve with homemade Tartar Sauce (see page 189) and lemon wedges.

Serves 4 / Prep 15 minutes (plus cooling) / Cook 1 hour 20 minutes / 500 kcal, 34g fat, 33g carbs, 11g protein

Chicken & Leek Pie

This is a delicious pie. You can make one big pie or individual pies, which are great for portion control! There is only pastry on the top, which obviously saves, not only some of the work, but some calories, too.

INGREDIENTS

50g (2oz) butter
3 leeks, washed really
  well and sliced
300g (10½oz) chestnut
  mushrooms
25g (1oz) plain flour, plus
  extra for dusting
300ml (10½fl oz) chicken
  stock
300g (10½oz) leftover
  cooked chicken (or cook
  and shred 2 chicken
  breasts)
2 tbsp wholegrain
  mustard
salt and pepper
320g (11oz) shop-bought
  puff pastry
1 egg, beaten

20cm (8in) pie dish

METHOD

1. Melt half of the butter in a large pan and soften the leeks for at least 10 minutes, then add the mushrooms and cook for 2 minutes until softened.

2. Remove the leeks and mushrooms from the pan and set aside.

3. Add the remaining butter to the pan along with the flour. Cook this, stirring all the time, for 1 minute. Now add the chicken stock, a little at a time, stirring constantly, until the flour and butter paste has dissolved into a thick sauce.

4. Simmer on a low heat and add the cooked chicken, leeks and mushrooms. Add the wholegrain mustard and season with salt and pepper. Spoon the chicken mixture into the pie dish and leave to cool.

5. Preheat the oven to 180°C (160°C fan/350°F/Gas 4).

6. Roll the puff pastry out on a floured work surface to the thickness of a £1 coin.

7. Lay the sheet of puff pastry over the top of the pie dish, pressing down around the sides to help seal it. Brush with egg wash.

8. Bake the pie in the oven for 1 hour until golden brown, then serve with lots of green veggies.

Serves 4 / Prep 10 minutes / Cook 1 hour 15 minutes / 760 kcal, 48g fat, 52g carbs, 26g protein

Quick Cheat's Steak & Mushroom Pasty

It is great to make your own shortcrust pastry, but I appreciate that you might not have the time or want to do that, so for this recipe I have used shop-bought pastry. It's a cheat, but totally worth it for this quick chip-shop classic.

INGREDIENTS

2 tbsp olive oil
1 large onion, finely chopped
250g (9oz) diced beef steak
250g (9oz) chestnut mushrooms, chopped (or use any white mushrooms)
2 garlic cloves, crushed
350ml (12fl oz) beef stock
2 bay leaves
1 tbsp cornflour (optional)
salt and pepper
500g (1lb 2oz) shop-bought shortcrust pastry
plain flour, for dusting
1 egg, beaten

baking tray, lined with baking parchment

METHOD

1. Heat the oil in a large frying pan, add the onion and cook for 5 minutes to soften. Add the steak and mushrooms and brown the meat on a higher heat for 10 minutes, then add the garlic and cook for another minute, being careful not to burn it.

2. Add the stock and bay leaves and simmer for about 30 minutes until reduced. If you need to thicken the sauce, mix the cornflour into 1 tbsp cold water and stir into the sauce. Season with salt and pepper and leave to cool. Remove the bay leaves.

3. Preheat the oven to 180°C (160°C fan/350°F/Gas 4).

4. Roll the pastry out on a lightly floured surface to the thickness of a £1 coin, then cut it into four circles, each about 20cm (8in) across.

5. On the right-hand side of each pastry circle, add one-quarter of the filling (leave a 2.5cm/1in gap from the right-hand edge). Egg wash the gap on the right-hand side of the filling and then fold the pastry over the filling from the left-hand side, giving you a pasty shape. Crimp the edges down together with your fingers or a fork.

6. Transfer the pasties onto the lined baking tray and brush with egg wash all over the top. Prick the centre of each pasty and bake for 30 minutes until golden. Serve.

Serves 12 / Prep 40 minutes (plus cooling and chilling) / Cook 35 minutes / 474 kcal, 31g fat, 31g carbs, 16g protein

Hidden Veg Sausage Rolls

Who doesn't like a sausage roll? However, the ones you find in the chippy (and in that lunchtime takeaway that has become famous for them) have never seen a vegetable. This recipe reduces the amount of sausage meat by bulking it up with lentils and veggies.

INGREDIENTS

1 tbsp olive oil
1 onion, finely chopped
150g (5oz) grated
  courgette
150g (5oz) grated carrot
2 garlic cloves, crushed
150g (5oz) grated eating
  apple
450g (1lb) good-quality
  sausage meat
400g can lentils, drained
  and rinsed
2 tbsp chopped sage
2 tbsp chopped flat leaf
  parsley
salt and pepper
plain flour, for dusting
500g (1lb 2 oz) shop-
  bought puff pastry
1 egg, beaten for
  brushing

METHOD

1. Heat the olive oil in a large frying pan, add the onion and cook for 5 minutes to soften. Add the courgette, carrot, garlic and apple and cook for another 5 minutes. Tip the cooked veg into a bowl and leave to cool (keep the pan to fry some of the mixture to try before baking).

2. When the veg is cool, add the sausage meat, drained lentils and chopped herbs and season (at this stage, you can fry off ½ tsp of the mixture to test the seasoning).

3. Dust a work surface with some flour and roll out the puff pastry into a large rectangle around the size of an A3 sheet of paper, about 40 x 25cm (16 x 10in). Cut it in half so you have two sheets about the size of A4 sheets of paper in landscape (the long end at the bottom).

4. Place half of the sausage mixture along the long bottom edge of one pastry sheet in a sausage shape. Then simply roll it up in the pastry, adding a little beaten egg to help seal the edges. Brush the sausage roll with beaten egg. Repeat with the remaining pastry sheet and sausage mixture.

5. Place in the fridge to firm up for 30 minutes–1 hour. (You can cut them into individual sausage rolls; freeze on a lined baking tray before popping into a container.)

6. Preheat the oven to 200°C (180°C fan/400°F/Gas 6).

7. Cook the sausage rolls on a baking tray in the oven for 30–35 minutes until golden brown. Serve hot or cold.

Serves 4 / 338 kcal, 13g fat, 34g carbs, 20g protein

Breaded Garlic Mushrooms

INGREDIENTS

100g (3½oz) plain flour
½ tsp paprika
½ tsp salt
1 tsp black pepper
100g (3½oz) dried breadcrumbs
100g (3½oz) Parmesan, finely grated
2 eggs, beaten
4 garlic cloves, crushed
200g (7oz) button mushroom

baking tray, lined with baking parchment

METHOD

1. Preheat the oven to 200°C (180°C fan/400°F/Gas 6).

2. Place the flour, paprika, salt and pepper in one bowl and mix well. Put the breadcrumbs and grated Parmesan in another bowl and mix. Put the beaten eggs and crushed garlic into a third bowl and mix well.

3. Now dip each mushroom into the flour, then the egg, then the breadcrumbs to coat, and place on the lined baking tray. Repeat this until they are all coated.

4. Place the baking tray into the oven and bake for 15 minutes, or until the mushrooms are crispy. Serve hot.

Serves 4 / 387 kcal, 18g fat, 28g carbs, 26g protein

Cheesy Courgette Fries

INGREDIENTS

2 eggs, beaten
1 tsp vegetable oil or low-calorie oil spray
70g (2½oz) dried breadcrumbs
5 tbsp finely grated Parmesan cheese
3 courgettes, trimmed, halved and cut into strips

baking tray, lined with baking parchment and greased with vegetable oil or low-calorie oil spray

METHOD

1. Preheat the oven to 200°C (180°C fan/400°F/Gas 6).

2. Place the beaten eggs in a shallow bowl. Mix together the breadcrumbs and Parmesan in another bowl.

3. Now dip a few courgette 'chips' into the beaten egg, shake off any excess, then roll them in the breadcrumbs mix. Place on the prepared baking tray. Repeat until all the chips are lightly covered.

4. Bake in the oven for 20 minutes until golden brown, then serve.

Serves 6–8 / 101 kcal, 4.6g fat, 12g carbs, 1.6g protein

Chip Shop Curry Sauce

INGREDIENTS

2 tbsp rapeseed oil or low-calorie oil
  spray
2 white onions, chopped
4 garlic cloves, crushed
2cm (¾in) piece fresh root ginger, grated
2½ tbsp mild curry powder
1 tsp ground turmeric
2 eating apples, cored and grated or finely
  chopped, or 100g (3½oz) raisins
400ml (14fl oz) chicken or vegetable stock
1 tbsp malt vinegar
2 tbsp cornflour mixed with 2 tbsp cold
  water

METHOD

1. Gently heat the oil in a large saucepan
   and soften the onions for 10 minutes.
   Add the garlic and ginger and fry for
   5 minutes without colouring them. Add
   the curry powder, turmeric and fruit
   and mix together for a minute – it's
   important that you cook the spices out.

2. Add the stock and vingear, giving it a
   stir and simmer gently for 30 minutes.

3. Add the cornflour mix while it is still on
   the heat, stirring all the time, and
   simmer for 2 minutes. If you need to
   loosen it, add 1–2 tbsp water.

4. Let it cool, then blend to get a smooth
   sauce. Cool and freeze any leftovers.

Serves 4 / 31 kcal, 2.8g fat, 1.1g carbs, 0.2g protein

Tartar Sauce

INGREDIENTS

4 tbsp mayonnaise
grated zest and juice of 1 lemon
1 tbsp capers, finely chopped
2 large gherkins, finely chopped
1 tbsp chopped dill
salt and pepper

METHOD

1. Mix the ingredients, season and serve.

Serves 4 / 54 kcal, 1.5g fat, 5.7g carbs, 3.0g protein

Mushy Peas

INGREDIENTS

200g (7oz) frozen peas
1 tbsp crème fraîche or plain yogurt
large handful of mint, chopped

METHOD

1. Cook the peas in boiling water for
   30–60 seconds. Drain, then crush the
   peas. Stir through the crème fraîche
   and mint.

Index

Thank You

Thank YOU for buying this book it really means a lot to me that you would part with your hard earned money to buy my book, I will never take that for granted and I am really grateful. I hope that in turn you really enjoy this book.

I have so many people I'd like to thank, firstly, for the huge privilege of being able to write my second cookbook, but also everyone that has helped me get to this position in my career.

I would like to thank everyone at DK Books for all their trust and support but special thanks should go to Mary-Clare Jerram, Stephanie Milner and everyone that worked so hard to make this book brilliant.

Thank you to Gee Charman, for your invaluable contribution and hard work.

I would also like to thank everyone who worked so hard to make the book look so great. Thank you to the amazing photography team that is Liz and Max Haarala Hamilton, great job guys. I had an amazing food stylist in Valerie Berry, which is arguably the most important job. Thank you to the really, really fun and original prop stylist Rachel Vere. Thanks to the brilliant, brilliant designer Jo Bell. And thanks Madge Foster for making me look presentable.

A huge thank you to everyone at DML, without them none of this would be possible, so thank you for your help and guidance – you all do such a great job. Thank you Jan, Borra, Louise and Tang.

I think it is fair to say that without all the amazing people at the BBC I wouldn't be doing any of this, so thank you for believing in me and letting me have my own adventure and new chapter in life. To work for the BBC is such an amazing opportunity and one I will always be grateful for and proud of.

A special thank you goes to: Charlotte Moore, Alison Kirkham, Carla Maria Lawson, David Bridley, Catherine Catton, Ricky Cooper and Lindsey Bradbury.

The first show I ever worked on and my introduction into the incredible world of TV was *Eat Well for Less?* and I owe so much to one particular person, Jo Scarratt-Jones – thank you for everything, for always having faith in me and for making this brilliant show that is such a joy to work on. I would also like to thank Fiona Gay and Kate Drysdale – you are both fantastic and have helped me immensely. I would like to thank my co-presenter and friend Gregg Wallace for all your advice and guidance – I will always remember and appreciate your kindness.

Friends and family are vitally important when you have a change in career, especially one that can be as daunting and different as this one, so I would like to thank my Mum and Dad for always being there for me, and to Alan and Gill, a big thank you for all you do for us.

To all my friends who always keep my feet firmly on the ground, and Ben, I missed you off last time so here you are! Cheers mate! And last but by no means least to my beautiful wife and partner Millie, you have done such an amazing job looking after our family. You challenge me to make me better every day and have supported me through thick and thin, I will forever be in your debt. Thank you for the amazing gift of our children who give me the constant motivation to never look back and keep moving forward. Kids, this book is for you, I am so proud to see how you are all growing into wonderful people, and how kind, funny and loving you are. You have given me and your Mum everything we could have ever dreamed of, so thank you.